971.5   Trueman, Stewart, 1911-
Tru   An intimate history of New Brunswick.
        Toronto, McClelland and Stewart, 1970.
            154 p.   illus., map.

RELATED
BOOKS IN   1. New Brunswick - Hist.   I. Title.
CATALOG
UNDER
                                79275

It CDN

An Intimate History of New Brunswick

An Intimate History of New Brunswick

by Stuart Trueman

114332

McClelland and Stewart Limited   *Toronto/Montreal*

0-7710-8606-7

The Canadian Publishers
McClelland and Stewart Limited,
25 Hollinger Road, Toronto 374

Printed and bound in Canada by
T. H. Best Printing Company Limited

Table of Contents

Author's Note

Warm thanks are due to the many sources of ready assistance in the preparation of this book. These include the New Brunswick Museum and the Saint John Regional Library, also several historians whose personal interest was greatly appreciated–Dr. George B. MacBeath, Fredericton, historical resources administrator for New Brunswick; Mr. L. Keith Ingersoll, history curator of the New Brunswick Museum; Mr. Emery LeBlanc, former editor of l'Evangeline, Moncton, and authority on the Acadian background; and Dr. W. Austin Squires, Fredericton, retired natural history curator of the New Brunswick Museum and author of historical works.

A Flag for all reasons

Whether a New Brunswicker happens to be of English or Acadian descent, or for that matter of German ancestry, he can feel that the province's vividly heraldic flag was custom-made for him. The gold lion rampant on a red field may be interpreted as adapted from the Arms of England, or from the armorial bearings of William the Conqueror, Duke of Normandy, or from the insignia of Brunswick, Luneburg and Westphalia in Germany, the British Royal Arms having been changed to include these armorial bearings upon the accession of the House of Hanover to the Throne of Great Britain in 1714. The ancient oared galley is, of course, multi-lingual–it's suggestive of the seafaring tradition of the old shipbuilding province. New Brunswickers think their boldly colourful flag, redolent of the medieval era of brave blazons and pennants, is the most striking in Canada.

1 The Great Migration

The rhythmic pounding of horses' hooves grew louder in the ears of the two rebel sentries. They knew from the tempo that their lieutenant's scouting party must be bringing back important tidings about the movements within General Cornwallis' encircled army. Leaning on their muskets, they looked out expectantly into the darkness.

Suddenly a troop of horsemen burst out of the underbrush, galloping past in the glarelight of the campfire so close that the stunned men could reach out and touch them, and went thundering on and away, leaving a fleeting impression of bright red coats and of a leader with cloak streaming in the breeze.

When a rebel lieutenant drew in a few minutes later to face the nervously upraised muskets, he could tell the men instantly who the chief will-o-the-wisp was. For the same dashing young Loyalist officer had been breaking the rebel vise night after night on forays in quest of food for the King's beleaguered forces. He was becoming a legendary figure, respected and reluctantly admired even by the most Tory-hating of Washington's men.

Later that evening the Loyalist troop took up positions around a wealthy plantation. Through the brightly lighted windows they could see young couples waltzing, and the sounds of string music and laughter warmed the cool evening air.

When the officer rapped the door-knocker, a startled black servant hurried off to bring the master.

"Your name, sir, and your business," said the planter,

staring not at the caller's face but at the scarlet military coat.

"John Coffin, major, New York Volunteers. Your home is surrounded by my men."

The planter visibly blanched.

"What do you want? I'm . . . I'm afraid you have me at a very considerable disadvantage. You see, my daughter has this day been married. We are having her wedding reception, which accounts for all the frivolity about."

"We need turkeys, hams and wine to feed my men, and as much as they can carry," the officer replied. "But there is no need to interrupt the gaiety of the occasion. If you will comply with our demands in good faith, we will go peaceably on our way."

The planter gladly did so. And as the provisions were being packed Major Coffin supped with the wedding party and waltzed with the bride, while the astonished guests gave them ample room on the dance floor.

As quickly as he had come, he vanished. And by dawn next morning "Coffin's Cavalry" was plunging back through the rebel lines amid a hail of bullets and then through the agreed point on the British perimeter, shouting the password ahead of them.

This was typical of Coffin's repeated brushes with death.

Descendant of a prominent English family that had lived at Alwington Manor in Devonshire since Norman times, and of Sir Tristram Coffin of the *Mayflower*, John Coffin was born in Boston but happened only by chance to take part in the Battle of Bunker Hill. As a boy he had gone to sea, becoming a master mariner at eighteen. His ship was landing British troops at Boston in 1775 when the strife erupted. Young Coffin exhibited such bravery with a navy unit at Bunker Hill that he was promptly made an ensign and transferred to the army.

Then began a storybook career of reckless derring-do. He formed a volunteer company of fifty men for the King's Orange Rangers, preferred always to fight rather than rest, saw action at Fort Montgomery, switched to the New York Volunteers, took part in the bloody hand-to-hand Battles of Hobkirk's Hill, South Carolina, and Eutah Springs in 1781.

Cornwallis heartily commended the audacity and resourcefulness of the young officer who fought at his side so often in "the most desperate encounters," but Major Coffin's promotions suddenly came to a halt. He was blacklisted for publicly exposing the cowardice of a natural son of King George III during a cavalry charge.

When Cornwallis capitulated at Yorktown in 1781, the elusive Major Coffin disappeared as if by witchcraft and the rebel army put a price of $10,000 on his head. He soon reappeared with the British forces retiring toward Charleston, North Carolina. Personally this suited him well – for at St. John's Island, Charleston, lived a lovely young woman he hoped to make his bride.

The fact that the American rebels still held Charleston did not deter him. He crept through their lines, was espied by a sentry, and sprinted for the Matthews residence as a hue and cry was raised behind him.

Within minutes there was a loud pounding on the Matthews' door. A rebel officer brushed aside the maid who answered, and before Ann Matthews could even rise from the divan he entered and announced: "A Redcoat has been seen near these grounds. We must search your house, ma'am."

"Please do," she said.

Ann heard the crash of heavy-boots exploring the upper floors. Then the officer returned to say: "Sorry, ma'am. We had to make sure. He's believed to be Major Coffin – a real bad one, a notorious Tory scoundrel. But he is not here."

"I'm greatly relieved to hear you say so," Ann smiled.

After the maid, peeking through the shutters, reassured her that "They're far down the street," Ann Matthews said: "You can come out now."

Suddenly her hoop skirts began to convulse, and out from under the lacey hem came an arm, and then another arm, and the dishevelled head and shoulders of a man, his face flushed as red as his tunic either with embarrassment or the discomfort of staying in a knees-doubled-up position for so long, or both. "Whew," he breathed as he clambered to his feet.

Major Coffin was to recall that unusual afternoon many times in his later life, and wonder how he ever managed to hide himself under a lady's skirts – he a heavily built man, six feet two inches in height. He was fortunate to live in the era of crinolines and not two centuries later.

For the sake of propriety, I am glad to be able to report that Major Coffin and Ann Matthews were married the same year – but not before he beat his way back to the British lines at New York, furtively crossing the Hudson and completely surprising many of his fellow officers who thought he had been captured and executed.

Major John Coffin was still only twenty-seven when he arrived as a United Empire Loyalist at the fledgling city of Saint John in September, 1783, accompanied by his wife and four black servants. It was a desolate panorama that greeted their eyes – a bleak rocky land covered sparsely by scrub cedar and spruce, and with army tents and lean-tos of evergreen boughs. As yet, four months after the landing of the first influx of 3,000 Loyalists, there were only a few rough log cabins.

Major Coffin was not staying here – he had bought 6,000 acres at Nerepis (Beaubear's Point) twelve miles up the St. John River. On this spacious tract stood a mansion which he named Alwington Manor but which became known to the neighbourhood as Coffin Manor.

Here the Major played affable host to the great and near-great as they travelled by boat or later by the new stagecoach route between Saint John and the provincial capital, Fredericton. Among his house guests in 1794 were Queen Victoria's father, the Duke of Kent, and his brother, the Duke of Clarence.

But it was not in Major Coffin's impulsive, pepper-tempered nature to settle down to indolent living, however gracious. He had to be up and at the next challenge. He never was one to hide his true feelings toward anyone, and if they didn't like it he was perfectly willing to settle matters with either sword or pistol.

Hardly had he arrived in New Brunswick before a flareup ensued between him and a Colonel Campbell, and in the resulting duel Major Coffin was wounded in the groin. He fought another duel with Captain Foy, stepson of Governor Carleton. Then when legislative member James Glennie of Sunbury virulently attacked Governor Carleton along with Edward Winslow, Coffin as a Kings County member felt he must call Glennie to account.

Here is how the Nova Scotia Royal Gazette of March

21, 1797, narrated the encounter, the initials being used so as not to incriminate the participants:

An affair of honour having lately happened in a neighbouring Province, between Col. C. – and Mr. G. – ; the following account of it (of the authenticity of which we are well assured) may not be unacceptable to our readers:

After the different overtures made by the friends of both parties had proved ineffectual, the gentlemen met in the woods opposite F——n, on Friday evening, the 24th of February, about five o'clock. The ground being marked out by the Seconds (Capt. M'L and Mr. S.) at 12 yards distance, they took their stands back to back; on receiving orders from the Seconds, they faced to the right, and fired together: – Col. C's shot went through Mr. G's thigh (a flesh wound.) Mr. S. communicated the circumstance to the Colonel, and asked if he was satisfied. Col. C. replied that he wished Mr. G. to make an apology for the words which had given offence. Mr. G. told him he was not much hurt, would keep his ground and exchange another shot, if he was not satisfied. Both the Seconds then observed that it was too late to demand an apology, upon which Col. C. –, in a manly manner, declared himself satisfied. Mr. G. afterwards told him, he did not mention it by way of apology, but now that the gentleman had declared himself satisfied, he could say upon his honour, he had no intention of conveying a personal insult in the language he made use of to Col. C. in the H. of A. Col. C. proposed they should meet half way, shake hands, and bury in oblivion all former animosities, which was accordingly done, and here the matter ended, and I am happy to think without any fatal consequences to either party.

After the "affair of honour," Mrs. Glennie declared to everyone within earshot that if her husband had not fought John Coffin she intended to herself – which possibly could have given him a lot more trouble.

The wonder of it is that considering the devil-may-care nature of his life, Major Coffin managed to live so long. Perhaps, he eventually mellowed slightly. He operated grist mills and sawmills, but never forgot his military background. In 1812, when war clouds again gathered over this country and the United States, he took command of the New Brunswick Fencibles. London's resistance to his advancement was finally broken down by his well-wishers – who at various times had been led by the Duke of Kent, Lord Cornwallis, Lord William Howe, Lord Rawson and the Marquis of Hastings – and at last in 1830 John Coffin was commissioned a general.

Despite his high rank, despite his proven ability to command men, there were some things General Coffin could not successfully do. One was to get his hired help up in the morning in time to light the fires and heat the house before he arose. He even tried putting out a glass of rum every night for the first farmhand up to tend the fires. It worked for a while; then the help caught on to the idea of getting up, drinking the rum and returning to bed well warmed while the general awoke to a freezing and cheerless mansion.

In later life he moved to a new house, which stood for a century, near Sagwa on the road to Fredericton. He imported fine livestock for the improvement of the Loyalist farms, and donated land to Trinity Church in Saint John.

Understandably, John Coffin took pride in the fact that of his three sons who entered the armed forces two became admirals in the Royal Navy and one a general in the British Army.

Today the highway traffic on the River Road between Saint John and Fredericton is busy and fast, and not one motorist in thousands ever notices two unassuming gravestones in full view under an old oak tree at Woodman's Point.

One says "Nath'l Coffin, Aged 15" and the other, simply, "General J. Coffin, Aged 87."

In their patriotic fervour, Americans today idealize the portrait of the marching trio of rebels in the image of whatever current movie stars whose noble profiles most closely resemble George Washington's. Now it is true that the revolutionary movement included dedicated colonists willing to risk their lives for their principles. But there was also the rabble who revelled in rioting and saw a chance to loot and burn at will – the criminals, anarchists and ne'er-do-wells.

At the start, the revolution was not a spontaneous general upswell of public fury. Had it been so, the British would have been promptly overwhelmed, as their total forces numbered no more than 45,000 troops, including 25,000 in the provincial regiments.

In fact the rebels were a distinct minority; the outright Loyalists also were a minority; most of the people remained uncommitted, waiting to see which way the war would go. Practically no one at that time seriously supposed America would sever her ties with Britain. The aim, before the intervention of France and Spain, was self-taxation and constitutional liberty.

The terrorist element had two contrasting effects. It intimidated many of the undecided into supporting the rebel cause and converted many others into staunch Loyalists. Many a public official was labelled royalist merely for trying to maintain order in the face of mob violence. A saying became popular: "Persecution made half the King's friends."

But the real orgy of barbarism began after the war — after the American government had pledged itself in the articles of peace to fair treatment of the Loyalists and restitution of confiscated estates and property. The individual states almost gleefully mocked this spirit of reconciliation. Vengeance against "traitors" was the catchword. "Hang them!" was the cry.

In Rhode Island the ultimate penalty for those dealing with the enemy was death and confiscation of estates. In Massachusetts anyone "denounced" could be arrested and sent to British-held territory; if he came back the automatic sentence would be death without benefit of clergy. Two Philadelphia men, Roberts and Carlisle, who stayed after the British evacuated the city, were marched to the gallows behind a cart, halters around their necks, and publicly hanged.

Loyalists soon became non-persons in many states, unable legally to sell or buy land, work, speak or write their opinions, collect debts by legal means, or seek the law's protection if physically attacked.

As the storm mounted, guffawing mobs who called themselves Sons of Liberty dragged prominent Tories through the streets, subjected them to "smoking" – confinement in a closed room before an open fire of green wood, with chimney blocked, made them sit on cakes of ice to cool their loyalty, tarred and feathered them, rode them on a rail through town, left them bound and gagged for days, warned old-time friends and neighbours not to dare speak to them, insulted and stoned their wives and daughters, poisoned their livestock, extorted their money and family silver in exchange for dubious protection, fired bullets into their homes, carted them about in wagons on public display, forced them to pay a forfeit as they entered each town, and in some places even drove Tory judges from the bench and abolished the courts.

This letter, written by a man in Newburg to a friend in Boston, October 22, 1783, expressed the mood:

The British are leaving New York every day. Last week there came one of the damned refugees from New York to a place called Walkill, in order to tarry with his parents, where he was taken into custody immediately. His head and eyebrows were shaved, he was then tarred and feathered, and a huge yoke put on his neck and a cowbell on it. Upon his head a very high cap of feathers was set, well plumed with soft tar, and a sheet of paper in front with a man drawn with two faces, representing Arnold and the Devil's imps, and on the back of it a card with the refugee or Tory driving her off.

In Boston, the wife and daughter of an absent Loyalist, Captain Fenton, were tarred and feathered and paraded around the streets.

Hamilton and Jay protested in vain. Washington tried, also without avail, to remind the mobs that these excesses might bring retribution. He pointed out that even though the victims had joined the British side after it had been declared treason to do so, they had not previously taken the oath of allegiance, nor entered the American service, so it could be said they had the privilege of choice. What, he asked, if the British took the same attitude toward natural-born subjects of Britain captured in the American service?

Sir Guy Carleton wrote from New York to Elias Boudinot of New Jersey:

The violence of the Americans, which broke out soon after the cessation of hostilities, increased the number of their countrymen who looked to me for escape from threatened destruction; but these terrors of late have been so considerably augmented that almost all within these lines conceive the safety both of their property and their lives to depend on their being removed by me, which renders it impossible to say when the evacuations can be completed.

Many a landowner, after his stables and barns had been burned down, and the lives of himself and his family threatened, would bid goodbye to his servants at the door of his colonial mansion, and climb into his carriage with his wife and children. Then, after a last look round at the serene, oak-lined grounds, the coachman would flick the whip and they would move onward, post-haste to New York. There they would board a British square-rigger, for the north woods and the land they had been promised – if not the promised land. Through the sympathetic good offices of Whitehall, they were entitled to 300 to 600 acres, plus more than a year's provisions or the equivalent in money; an allowance of serviceable clothing and medicine, mill-stones, ironwork for a grist mill, or needed items for a sawmill; nails, spikes, hoe, axe, spade, shovel, plow-irons, musket, powder and ball; also window-glass. Plus the prospect of the back-breaking life of a pioneer.

Altogether 100,000 persons were hounded out of the thirteen colonies, 35,000 to 40,000 settling in Nova Scotia, which then included New Brunswick.

New England towns were stripped of prominent citizens – Saltonstalls, dePeysters, Pepperells, Fanuels, Quincys, Royals, deLanceys, Hutchinsons, Sewalls, Winslows, Winthrops, Chaloners, Princes, Sears, Waterburys. Garrisons joined the exodus. Little wonder that northeastern Americans today find so many similarities in Maritime surnames.

When General Gage evacuated Boston, so did 1,100 of Boston's residents, including 102 members of the council, commissioners, customs authorities and other officials, and eighteen clergymen. Among the refugees were one hundred Harvard alumni.

Today the metropolis would hardly notice the departure of 1,100 people but at that time Boston's remaining population was only 15,000. As a matter of fact, Saint

John, which was a mere trading post until the Loyalist deluge came, found itself with 5,000 souls braving the harsh winter of 1783-84. Overnight the tiny wilderness outpost had grown to one-third the size of Boston.

Anti-Loyalist fervour reached such fever pitch that Dr. John Calef's family in Ipswich, Massachusetts, began to fear for their safety. He had been away two years in England, negotiating unsuccessfully on behalf of Penobscot Loyalists who hoped the final boundary line would keep them under the Union flag. During the war he had been ship's surgeon on a British sloop commanded by Captain Henry Mowat, who destroyed Falmouth (now Portland) in retaliation for the townspeople's cruelty to the Tories. Now Ipswich seethed with ugly talk of wreaking revenge on Dr. Calef.

Mrs. Calef, a resourceful woman, chartered a sloop, hired men to load the family mahogany highboys, lowboys and other furniture aboard, and sailed for Saint John with her children. They straggled ashore in a blizzard at nearby Red Head, and were helped by sailors to reach the port town. Equally resourceful Captain David Mowat, a Loyalist fugitive to whom little Hetty Calef had carried food in the forest, chartered a schooner, sailed up and down the coast and succeeded in intercepting the ship bringing Dr. Calef home.

They beached the schooner on the Maine coast in a storm, made their way furtively along the shore at night, hiding by day, wading swamps and swimming rivers. When they finally stumbled into the New Brunswick settlement of St. Andrews, not even their former friends noticed them – which may testify to the effectiveness of their disguise as an Indian and his squaw.

There are still family mementoes in St. Andrews of this exploit, for Captain David Mowat stayed to marry, two years later, pretty eighteen-year-old Miss Mehitabel Calef – the same little Hetty who had been sent to carry her mother's food baskets to him in the forest glade because no one would suspect a child of treason.

But the cruelty in this cruellest kind of war – a civil war – was not confined by any means to the American side.

The British could hardly take pride in Colonel David

Fanning who took such sadistic delight in chronicling in detail how he hunted down and killed revolutionaries. He was the nemesis of North Carolina rebels, leading his band of cavalry into towns on seemingly impossible missions – like the time they captured the governor himself and members of his council.

It does not require a psychologist to pin-point at least one reason for Fanning's brutality and vindictiveness. He had suffered agonies at the hands of the rebels. Three times he had escaped from imprisonment, the last after sawing his naked body free from the chains that stapled him to the floor of his cell and fleeing with one leg still dragging eight pounds of metal – and with two bullets fired by guards embedded in his back.

Revenge, then, to Colonel David Fanning was sweet; and he made it last deliciously. He was proud of such exploits as when he sought out a Chatham wedding, stood the members of the bridal party against a wall, searched them and accused one young man of being a belligerent rebel. Then, when the fellow tried to run away, he rendered the *coup de grace* by firing both pistols at his breast after one of his men had winged him in the shoulder, spinning him around.

Listen to Colonel Fanning exult as he relishes the sheer joy of killing:

We set out for one Balfour's plantation . . . he endeavored to make his escape, but we soon prevented him . . . the first ball he received through one of his arms and ranged through his body, the other through his neck, which put an end to his committing any more ill deeds. We also wounded another of his men, then proceeded to Colonel Collier's . . . on our way we burned several rebel houses . . . it was late before we left there [the colonel's]. . . . He made his escape having received three balls through his shirt, but I took care to destroy the whole of his plantation.

I then pursued our route and came to one Captain John Bryan's . . . I told him if he would come out of the house I would give him parole, which he refused . . . I immediately ordered the house to be set afire . . . as soon as he saw the flames of the fire increasing he called out to me and desired me to spare his house for his wife and children.

I immediately answered him that if he would walk out his house and property should be saved ... and when he came out he said, "Here, damn you, here I am." With that he received two balls, the one through his head and the other through his body ... he came out with his gun cocked and sword at the same time.

This then was Colonel David Fanning, who was later to join the Loyalist migration to Saint John and, ignored by most patrons, sit in the Exchange Coffee House hobnobbing over drinks with another infamous King's man, General Benedict Arnold.

Even as Americans glorify their patriots, many Canadians imagine the typical Loyalist to be the resolute man in a well-known life insurance company's calendar painting – strong chin up, musket over shoulder, wife by side, looking towards Destiny.

This certainly expresses the spirit. But in reality the coming of the Loyalists was a very human event, beset by all kinds of everyday human problems like fog and rain, measles and baby-squalling. The Loyalists didn't have time to think of themselves as heroic because they were too busy wondering how to survive and what kind of a reception they'd get from the Indians.

Even before leaving New York on April 26 they had become involved in very human wrangles. Many angrily thought that fifty-five prominent Loyalists who had petitioned Sir Guy Carleton for 5,000 acres each in Nova Scotia, in consideration of their losses and their services to the Crown, were overstating things. A counter-petition claimed that the fifty-five, in easy circumstances, hadn't suffered much at all.

Back of the squabbling was the fear that if influential refugees grabbed off huge lots of the best land, the ordinary Loyalist might get short shrift.

However, they sailed away in high hopes, and it must have made a brave and stirring sight to see the twenty square-riggers of the Loyalist Spring Fleet bearing out of New York to begin the great migration.

The *Aurora, Camel, Grand Duchess of Russia, Hope, Lady's Adventure, Mars, Sovereign, Spencer, Spring, Union:* one by one the big transports headed majestically out to sea, carrying 3,000 men, women and children away from civilization and northward to a land which, although few knew it, was as bleak and unbroken and forbidding as today's lonely coves on the coast of Labrador.

In one mass disembarkation they were to double the English-speaking population of what is now New Brunswick.

Despite the hearty booming salutes of the welcoming cannon at Fort Howe on the rocky hilltop overlooking Saint John harbour, despite the fact that a few scattered people on shore were waving, the settlers were appalled by their first view of their future home. It was nothing but wilderness, scruffy wilderness at that.

Few preparations had been made for them. Before the Loyalists could be landed from the overcrowded ships, brush had to be cut away from Upper Cove (later Market Slip) so the first tents and hurricane houses of sails could arise. Most passengers stayed on board their ships several days, the general movement ashore finally starting May 18 and inscribing that day forever in history as Loyalist Day.

By a quirk of human nature, few people broke down and wept on their arrival. But when they saw the transports hoisting their sails to return to New York, when they realized the irrevocability of their landing in this crude environment, strong wills weakened for a moment. As one young woman later recalled: "I climbed to the top of Chipman's Hill and watched the sails disappear, and such a lonely feeling came over me that, although I had not shed a tear through all the war, I sat down on the damp moss with my baby in my lap and cried."

She was to become the grandmother of Sir Leonard Tilley, a Father of Confederation. It was he, incidentally, who scanned his Bible and suggested the word "Dominion" for Canada.

Luckiest of the migrants were those aboard the *Union*, which led the fleet into port. They immediately went up-river exploring in a small sloop, thought first of settling on Belleisle Bay because the timbered highlands there had not been burned by the Indians, then decided on Kingston Creek. They tented for weeks, were supplied with moose steaks by Indians who greeted them with the shout "We all one brother!" – an echo of the great pow-wow at Fort Howe five years before – and had their log cabins snugly built and occupied by November. This was a triumph of co-operation, for the pioneers had to drag their logs by hand as they had neither horses nor oxen.

Soon they erected Trinity Anglican church, which today is the oldest church still standing and one of the oldest buildings in New Brunswick. For ninety years there was family continuity in the rectorship – first Reverend James Scovil of Waterbury, Connecticut, then his son, Reverend Elias Scovil, and his grandson, Reverend William Elias Scovil.

By contrast, look at the Saint John Loyalists. Many soon felt that their original misgivings were all too well founded. Though the British government was sympathetic, numerous details had been badly mishandled. Governor Parr in Halifax was good enough to lend his name to the new city on the east side of the harbour – "Parrtown" – a name he ascribed to "feminine vanity," meaning his wife suggested it. But he didn't lend his presence. He didn't come near his namesake community. The Loyalists felt remote from higher officialdom. It was not surprising that they began to agitate to separate this mainland Sunbury County from Nova Scotia and set up a new province. This was done the next year, and Parrtown and Carleton across the harbour were combined in 1785 into Saint John, to make it the first incorporated city in British North America.

Because many of the Loyalists who intended to go up-river found themselves ensnarled in red tape, a large number decided to draw lots in the city itself and then found those lots gradually shrinking to one-sixteenth of their original size as more Loyalists kept flooding into Parrtown.

The Summer Fleet brought a further mass influx of 2,000. Among 250 passengers on the *Two Sisters* were Sarah Schofield Frost and her husband William, the "Billy" Frost who electrified Stamford by his reckless boldness. As a staunch Loyalist he had been blacklisted for death if he ever returned to Connecticut. But return he did in 1781, guiding an armed expedition which secreted itself in a swamp one Saturday night. Next morning they surrounded and captured a vociferous "patriot," Reverend Doctor Mather, and his whole congregation. The raiders selected forty-eight of the most strident patriots, packed them into boats and delivered them behind the British lines at

Lloyd's Neck on Long Island to the whoops and catcalls of Stamford Loyalists who had been dispossessed by their accusing fingers.

Picture colonial families who had lived in spacious and stately homes. Then imagine the Frosts and six other households all jammed into one cabin of the *Three Sisters*, spending three weeks on board even before the flotilla sailed! Any mother of today can feel kinship with Sarah Frost, twenty-eight, when she penned in her diary: ". . . there is great confusion in the cabin. You can bear it pretty well through the day, but at night one child cries in one place and one in another while we are getting them to bed. I think sometimes I will go crazy."

The Summer Fleet, too, met blustery gales and often the thirteen ships, two brigs and a frigate, were enveloped in fogs so thick no vessel could see another – "they rang their bells and fired guns all the morning to keep company with one another."

But the Frosts remained cheerful. The definition of the opportunist is the man who finding himself in hot water takes a bath; the Frosts promptly got out a mug when marble-sized hailstones fell, and made ice-cold punch. They played crib with another couple. When the ships were becalmed, the men dropped lines over the side and hauled in gleaming mackerel and cod. Even a flare-up of measles among the children failed to dismay the parents overmuch, because the long stay on shipboard that had extended more than a month was nearing its end.

At Parrtown Billy Frost went ashore and brought back a plump salmon; others returned with "pea vines with blossoms on them, gooseberries, spruce and grass." Wrote Sarah Frost: "They say this is to be our city," and later, after a brief excursion on shore, "it is, I think, the roughest land I ever saw. We are all ordered to land tomorrow and not a shelter to go under."

The Frosts, and others like them, had tough inner fibre. Sarah Frost didn't go crazy as she predicted. She coped with emergencies, and drew strength from each success for the next crisis. Just five weeks after landing she gave birth to a daughter, Hannah, second child born in Parrtown. (The first was Ann, daughter of Thatcher Sears of Connecticut, born in a tent near the landing place soon after the disembarkation.)

It isn't easy today to visualize the uncompromising harshness of the 1783 scene. For instance, if the first Loyalists didn't have horses or oxen, did they wheel or drag their goods along the streets? But there were no streets. True, street lines had been run and trees cut down, but all the stumps were to remain for several years. The only way to move possessions from Upper Cove to Lower Cove in the South End was by boat to the shore, and then on your back. For several years there was not one mile of good road in the province, so the Loyalists had to use the same travel routes as the Indians – the broad rivers and the portages where you toted your birchbark canoe on your head.

The Fall Fleet disgorged another 1,200 settlers, mostly American Loyalist soldiers from disbanded regiments. Among them were the residue of the Royal Guides and Pioneers, New Jersey Volunteers, New York Volunteers, King's American Dragoons, Queen's Rangers, King's American Regiment, Pennsylvania Loyalists, DeLancey's 1st and 2nd Battalions, and the seventy-five survivors of the Maryland Loyalists, whose transport, *Martha*, was wrecked en route with the loss of ninety-nine passengers. These were allocated lands along the river from Fredericton to and beyond Woodstock. Farther up were to be the tracts for the Prince of Wales American Regiment, the 1st and 3rd New Jersey Volunteers, Arnold's American Legion, the Loyal American Regiment – all according to a grand strategic scheme of settling veterans where they could be hurriedly mobilized near the border, in case of a later invasion. But the season was so late that few even attempted to go so far north.

Their plight seared the conscience of Edward Winslow. He wrote to Ward Chipman:

I saw all those Provincial Regiments, which we have so frequently mustered, landing in this inhospitable climate in the month of October, without shelter and without knowing where to find a place to reside. The chagrin of the officers was not to me so truly affecting as the poignant distress of the men. Those respectable sergeants of Robinson's, Ludlow's, Cruger's, Fanning's – once hospitable yeomen of the Country – addressed me in language that almost murdered me as I heard it:

"Sir, we have served all the war, Your Honour is witness how faithfully. We were promised land; we expected you had obtained it for us. We like the country — only let us have a spot to call our own."

But meanwhile the early-arrived Loyalists, in a tremendous burst of industriousness, had completed 1,500 dwellings at Parrtown and Carleton before winter blizzards struck.

These weren't quite as pretentious as the estates they had vacated on the Hudson and Susquehanna. Incongruously, the typical humble one-room log cabin, its cracks jammed with moss and clay, roof formed by shorn poles overlaid with sheets of bark, daylight filtering through one small window, might at the same time boast a rich red mahogany dresser, an imposing grandfather clock, glowing silver plate and candle-snuffers, crystal, and a massive leather-covered Bible.

In the drawers of the dresser and hanging from the log wall was finery that seemed somehow out of place in rough-hewn Parrtown — lovely shimmering silk gowns, a velvet-lined, blue damask frock coat, knee-breeches of gold nankeen, white silk stockings, blue morocco slippers with oversize silver buckles.

Unfortunately many Loyalists in their haste to leave the thirteen colonies had overlooked the practical heirlooms they needed most. As a result, numerous cabins in Saint John possessed only primitive beds made from four poles, with strips of basswood bark woven between the poles. There might not even be chairs or tables; these at the outset were luxury items. After all, a man could eat anywhere, even standing; to sleep he needed a bed of some sort.

But the Loyalists who got themselves ensconced within four walls were the fortunate ones — far more so than the late arrivals who managed only to pitch canvas shelters before winter savagely gripped the landscape. They suffered intensely from the icy cold in tents thatched with spruce boughs and banked with snow. When it rained, it soaked up into their beds. Many women and children died of malnutrition and exposure.

Even the officer commanding the final transports in December, Lieutenant John Ward of the Loyal Americans, had to take whatever shelter he could get – his son John Jr. was born in an army tent whose door flapped ceaselessly in winter's chill blasts sweeping Barrack Square.

The Loyalist women who attempted to go on to St. Anne's (Fredericton) in late autumn had to winter with their families in forest glades en route, with the frozen ground for a floor, the only heat coming from circular field-stone fireplaces. Night after night mothers heated boards and stones to hold against their infants, or pressed them desperately to their bodies.

Ironically, when the snows melted, numerous Loyalist families were kept alive by the discovery of patches of wild-growing beans, white beans surcharged by a black cross, planted decades before by Acadians. Thus New Englanders who had driven the Acadians out of Fredericton were saved by the foresight of the people they dispossessed.

At St. Andrews, closer to the present border of Maine, Loyalists were confronted with an added hazard. Many had moved from the Penobscot River country when they realized it would be within the new republic's borders. Some at Castine had taken their houses apart, section by section, and loaded them on ships and barges for transport to St. Andrews – Canada's first prefabricated housing. (One reassembled home is still standing on Montagu Street.) But they found American agents hovering about St. Andrews declaiming that the final boundary would be drawn much nearer Saint John – probably at the Maga-guadavic River, which the agents contended was the original St. Croix – and so they should hie themselves off American soil fast or face the consequences.

The Loyalists, after their countless vicissitudes, were too resilient to be intimidated. They stood their ground. One was a surveyor, John (Mahogany) Jones, who despite repeated threats kept on peacefully marking trees along the St. Croix. Some time previously he had opened a letter from Washington, warning the inhabitants, but had hidden it away and mentioned it to no one.

Stirred up by American agent Colonel John Allan, Indians seized John Jones and imprisoned him in an English house. That ended the surveying – until that same evening when, as a current account says, Mahogany Jones "made his elopement" and went on marking trees. The Indians let him alone, as Colonel Allan had by now departed.

It's not altogether surprising if Mahogany Jones – nicknamed for his bronzed, sun-tanned complexion – was so imperturbable as to baffle any attempt to incarcerate him. When the war broke out, this surveyor for the Plymouth Company on the Kennebec had been arrested as a Loyalist and imprisoned in Boston. He escaped to Quebec, was appointed a captain in Roger's Rangers and his daring troop soon became known as "Jones' Rangers." They revelled in danger. An old enemy of Mahogany Jones was Colonel Cushing, high sheriff of Lincoln, and in 1780 Jones' Rangers came charging through Kennebec County, broke into the high sheriff's house at night and carried him off in his nightgown to the British at Penobscot.

Like many a Loyalist, it may be noted, Mahogany Jones didn't remain in British America. When hostility at home cooled in later years, he went back to the Kennebec and died in Augusta. Time finally tempered the attitude of Americans toward the Tories – even as time also ameliorated the attitude of the British in New Brunswick toward the returning Acadians.

Very much a member of the Establishment in St. Andrews was Dr. William Paine of Worcester, Massachusetts. He had been a close personal friend of John Adams, later President Adams of the United States, and other leading figures in the revolution.

Often, as he trod the rutted, red-soil streets of the seaside town, Dr. Paine winced at the memory of that dinner at his old home – the time when he proposed a toast to the health of the King, and for an awful moment he thought some of his independence-minded guests were not going to comply because they were avidly whispering among themselves. But John Adams must have advised them to, because they all arose and raised up their brandies.

"To His Britannic Majesty," Dr. Paine intoned.

"To His Britannic Majesty," echoed the chorus.

They drained their glasses.

Then up got John Adams, smiling.

"I wish to propose a toast," he said, "to His Satanic Majesty – the Devil."

Momentary silence. . . . Dr. Paine could feel his ears burning at the insult; he knew his face was flushed.

But Mrs. Paine was equal to the occasion. In a room tense and still, she spoke toward her husband: "My dear," she said, "as the gentleman has been so good to drink to the health of the King, let us by no means refuse to drink to *his* friend."

Dr. Paine served his new homeland far-sightedly. He won a seat as a member for Charlotte County in the first New Brunswick elections, became first clerk of the House, was a leader in the move to establish a provincial academy at Fredericton. This evolved into today's rapidly developing University of New Brunswick, which prides itself on being Canada's oldest university.

Oddly, President John Adams seems to have had more close friends in Loyalist New Brunswick than in the entire republic he espoused.

You can find others in the Old Loyalist Burying Ground, a quiet, tree-shaded square in uptown Saint John – a cemetery so venerated by the original settlers that when Common Council decided to cut off interments on May 1, 1848, because the place was filling up, several ailing old Loyalists prayed they would die before the deadline.

One notable vault is the resting place of the Honourable James Putnam, Harvard alumnus, last Attorney-General under His Majesty in Massachusetts and the most eminent lawyer of his era in that American Province. John Adams studied law in Mr. Putnam's office, and resided with the Putnam family. When he arrived in New Brunswick, Mr. Putnam became a member of His Majesty's Council and a judge of the Supreme Court.

In the same vault repose the remains of Jonathan Sewell, also a Harvard alumnus, also a former Attorney-General of Massachusetts, also a close friend of John Adams. The president-to-be respected Sewell's brilliant scholarly attainments, his quick and perceptive mind, his wit and eloquence.

In fact, it was Jonathan Sewell who strove to persuade John Adams it would be a serious mistake to attend the first Continental Congress. They argued heatedly as they strolled the heights at Portland, and it was then that Adams uttered the words that have gone down in American history: "The die is now cast; I have now passed the Rubicon; sink or swim, live or die, survive or perish with my country is my unalterable decision."

After that strained parting they did not see each other again for many years – not until 1788, five years after the Loyalists' arrival.

Sewell's son, Jonathan Jr., was a great source of pride to him. The boy indisputably had talent. He went to England with his parents and brother at the evacuation of Boston in 1776 and remained there at school when his father and mother sailed to Saint John.

One day in Bristol, England, both Jonathan and Stephen Sewell participated in a dramatic performance that drew accolades from reigning tragedienne, Dame Sarah Siddons. To young Jonathan she penned these ecstatic lines:

The world is dull, and seldom gives us cause
For joy, surprise or well-deserved applause;
Young Heaven-sent Sewell; behold! in thee
Sufficient causes for all the three.
Thy rising genius managed Cato's part
To charm away and captivate the heart;
'Tis rare for boys like thee to play the man –
There are few in years who nobly can;
But thou, a youth of elegance and ease,
In Cato's person, to perform and please,
Hast common youth and manhood both undone,
And proved thyself Dame Nature's chosen son.

Later the youth journeyed to Saint John and became New Brunswick's first law student. He studied in the office of Ward Chipman, yet another Harvard alumnus who had been British deputy master muster-general in New York, now Solicitor-General of New Brunswick, and would become a Supreme Court judge. Young Jonathan lived with the Chipmans till his family came.

His doting father could hardly wait to reach Saint John himself, as these excerpts from a letter to Ward Chipman show: "To all you say about my dear son Jonathan, I have only to answer that every line drew from me a tear of pleasure. Fond fathers, you know (or will know soon, for I hear you are in the road to matrimony) are fools. . . . My wishes, which hitherto have been humble, have now grown ambitious, and terminate in nothing short of a set down at St. John . . . I want to spend the remaining days of my pilgrimage in the newest New Jerusalem – the City of St. John. . . ."

Young Jonathan moved to Quebec in 1791, became

Solicitor-General of that colony, Attorney-General, eventually Chief Justice. In 1796 he married an heiress, daughter of Chief Justice William Smith of Lower Canada. They had twenty-two children.

Surprisingly, the Jonathan Sewell home is still standing at the corner of Duke and Ludlow streets, Saint John West. A large square wooden building, the once patrician residence – one of the oldest surviving dwellings in Saint John – is now a rooming house. It has a four-pitch roof that comes up to a point, "nosed" siding (like clapboards with a waterfall edge along the bottom), a beautiful fanlight over the front door, "sidelights" of numerous panes lead-framed in graceful designs.

Indoors you are struck by many authentic Loyalist attributes – the eight big fireplaces, the very small round brass doorknobs on the original doors and large rectangular brass surface locks below the knobs, the huge hand-hewn timbers in the basement, the wooden pegs that hold the beams at the joints, the fieldstone and mortar walls, the curious fact that the stone chimney-base also contains large square timbers, the extremely steep and narrow winding stairs to the attic, and the baffling attic beams that are papered with 1837 newspapers, apparently on the theory that this would preserve the wood.

The present owner, Ian Donald, a school-teacher and an antiquarian by hobby, has been trying to restore the old building. He admits the house puzzles him. Its design seems more or less contemporary with Saint John's up-town Loyalist House (1817), a four-pitch-roofed public landmark, notable for the huge brick cooking-fireplace in its kitchen, its kitchen closets and original heavy pots and pans and cranes.

"But," he points out, "documents show this has been known through history as the Sewell house, which would place it before 1796, when Jonathan Sewell Senior died."

Just a few doors up Duke Street West is the home of Saint John's first mayor – Ludlow House, otherwise known as Carleton House, Government House, Bentley House – but it has been made into a multi-occupancy house now and it has become unrecognizable. Here, on the site of a former charming French garden and orchard, Hon. Gabriel G. Ludlow built a fine home that did justice to his position – a position enhanced when he became President and

Commander-in-Chief of the province on the departure of Governor Thomas Carleton for England in 1803.

A glittering state dinner was given here in 1794 in honour of His Royal Highness the Duke of Kent, father of Queen Victoria. It was a sumptuous repast, attended by many American Loyalist commanders including Mayor Ludlow, formerly of Hampstead, New York, the man who raised the 3rd Battalion of DeLancey's Brigade.

In fact, there are numerous old houses on the west side of Saint John Harbour, in contrast to the east side. The reason is that the western area was spared disastrous fires. The city's central peninsula was swept by one conflagration after another, culminating in the Great Fire of 1877 that left 13,000 homeless. The only thing that saved part of central Saint John was the great hundred-foot width of hilly King Street.

Many of the Loyalists still yearned for their old homes – homes that now seemed no more than dreamlike memories. Once the mob hysteria in the new republic had subsided, some wanted to go back to stay. Others merely wanted to see relatives again.

Among these was Loyalist Charity Newton from Rhode Island, who had married Ebenezer Smith and settled in Kings County. She brought along her baby, a basket, and a barrel of mixed fruits and vegetables to show her family that she didn't live on roots and snared rabbits. But new stresses were developing between the United States and England, which was now at war with France, and passengers from Saint John could land at only a few authorized ports. It was frustrating to Charity when the ship found itself drifting becalmed in Long Island Sound. She could recognize landmarks, even the house of an old neighbour, yet she could not leave the ship. The captain was kindly if gruff. "I cannot order my seamen to row you ashore," he said, "because it would contravene the regulations. However," he went on, "I am now going below to work on my log, and if you persuade them to do so without my knowledge, I cannot prevent it."

Charity, her baby, basket and barrel thus arrived at her old home to find the house vacated, but cows still in the barn. Knowing that someone would eventually come to feed and milk the herd, she and the baby slept with the cows. The next day she was reunited with her family in their new home – only to discover, after all her arduous travel, that her mother was now mentally ill and did not recognize her long-gone daughter.

Embarking on an English ship at New York for the return voyage, Charity was hardly out to sea again when a sail slowly grew on the horizon. "It's a Frenchman!" the master growled, adding with a sigh, "and I am carrying silver specie."

"Will they take us as prisoners to France?" Charity asked.

"No, ma'am," he reassured her. "That would be too much bother. The procedure is as formal as a pirouette. They will escort us to the nearest neutral port, which is back to New York, and claim the usual ransom." Tight-lipped, he went on: "But I begrudge them the prize of silver specie. I should cast it overboard."

If Loyalist women were anything they were resourceful; they had to be. Quickly summoning all the female passengers, Charity put them to work sewing silver coins between two of her petticoats, taking care not to place any so close together they might jangle. The women had just got her metal-studded petticoats loaded on to her torso when a cannon shot was heard and the ship signalled its surrender.

Charity carried her bulky burden tolerably well on the trip back to New York until she saw the single gangplank extending from the ship to the wharf. She staggered at the sight. The French captain bowed gallantly. He understood in an instant. He ordered his men to add more planks. Then, with a French officer assisting her on each side, Charity, heavy with specie, stumbled ashore and thanked them all for their helpfulness to a lady in her condition.

Did a rough-and-ready life of unaccustomed toil soon turn the Loyalist patricians into coarse hillbillies? Apparently not. In 1799 – sixteen years after the Loyalists' arrival – Scott Brothers of Greenock sent their mode-conscious, twenty-one-year-old younger brother, Christopher, out to New Brunswick to build ships. He wrote back that the quality of the local hardwood and pine was superlative – also that the town of Saint John was not the unkempt and law-defying outpost he had anticipated, but "uncommonly orderly and well conducted" and the ladies were "remarkable well dressed, clean, neat and affecting a degree of fashionability surprising in such a place."

Nearly half a century later Mrs. F. Beaven published a book in London, *Sketches and Tales Illustrative of Life in the Backwoods of New Brunswick, North America*. She described the people as "a most indescribable genus, those bluenoses." She spoke of "the traces of descent from the Dutch and French blood of the United States being mingled with the independent spirit of the American and the staunch firmness of the 'Britisher,' as they delight to call themselves, showing their claim to it by the most determined hatred of the Yankees, whose language and features they yet retain. Yet these differing qualities blend to form a shrewd, active, intelligent and handsome people – intelligence and strong sense to a far greater degree than could be found in persons of the same class in England."

Mrs. Beaven commented, "Many of the children are perfectly beautiful, but the cherub beauty changes soon, and the women particularly look old and withered while still young in years. Even the children of immigrants are much handsomer than those born at home."

Predictably, North American democracy startled her. She had difficulty getting accustomed to the spectacle of the squire yoking his oxen, a major selling turkeys, the member for the county cradling buckwheat.

Nevertheless, she concluded that much of this was productive of good. Her reasoning: through the intermingling of classes the graces and politeness of the higher circles would be imparted to those with whom they conversed.

She remarked: "An air or refinement is native to a New Brunswicker . . . rudeness and vulgarity in glaring forms one never meets from them." On the other hand, "Odd and inquisitive ways may be thought impertinent, and require both time and patience to be rightly understood."

On the debit side, she noted "New Brunswick may be forgiven for whispered tales that float about, of corn being reaped and wood being felled on the Sabbath day, and of sacred rites being dispensed with." And this penetrating observation about new Canadians came from Mrs. Beaven, who, though she little suspected it, must have been by then a good New Brunswicker at heart:

Many of the emigrants, although better off than they could possibly expect to be at home, yet keep railing at the country. . . . The Yorkshireman talks of nothing but the "white cakes and bag puddings" of old England, regardless of the pumpkin pies and buckwheat pancakes of New Brunswick; and one old lady from Cornwall (where they say the Devil would not go for fear of being transformed into a pasty) revenges herself on the country by making pies of everything, from apples and mutton down to parsley, and all for the memory of England; while perhaps, were she there, she might be without a pie.

Six years later, in 1851, an English author using the byline "Mackworth Shore," which sounds so implausible it might be his name, arrived in Saint John by ship from Boston. At Eastport several Maine and New Brunswick passengers came aboard, and he dwelt in his book on their "fine figure, fresh complexion and winning expressions," contrasted with the "haggard, careworn, pallid, ugly faces of Massachusetts." Of his continuing trip: "If I was struck by the beauty of the Maine females in one steamer, I was astounded in St. John; in fact, it is notorious for the beauty of its women."

One other thing struck him about the "bluenoses of New Brunswick" – their lack of inhibitions. They appeared "free from the cold reserve which strangers attribute to the English" and they readily and good-naturedly talked with him on the steps of his hotel, "even though" – he remarked in surprise – "they had not been introduced to me."

2 Ghosts and Other Apparitions

"I was never so frightened in my life," said the silvery-haired old lady with the piercing dark eyes, and you knew Mrs. Fred McKillop really meant it.

She was speaking of the spring day in 1951 when she saw the Lake Utopia monster. The recollection was hardly calculated to steady an eighty-six-year-old woman's nerves. "The lake was so still and beautiful – as smooth as glass. I was looking at it with two of my grandchildren.

"Suddenly the water began to boil and made waves that came right in to us on shore. Then a huge blackish creature broke through the surface – its head and part of its body – threshing and churning . . . and it began to move through the water!

"I was so terrified I took the children, ran into the cabin and locked the door."

After a while, realizing it wasn't pursuing them, she emerged and watched it travelling up and down the broad, deep, seven-mile-long lake.

Though herself a resident of nearby St. George in southern New Brunswick, she had never heard of the Lake Utopia monster until she described it to others of the family when they arrived for supper.

It was a relief to Mrs. McKillop to learn that two groups of anglers had also seen the eerie spectacle that day – but they gave her little support. One group had been exuberantly partying and preferred to forget what they saw. The other didn't notice the churning, but had been surprised to see what seemed to be an instant sandbar appear in the lake. But the inquiring grandmother found no lack of previous sightings. The Lake Utopia monster had showed itself from time to time for nearly one hundred years. Presumably there had been more than one sea serpent – or this was an especially durable specimen as monsters go.

Historian Dr. W. F. Ganong wrote in 1891 that residents of the district had often espied its dark-red head and neck thrusting above the agitated waves – "as big around as a small hogshead."

One of his informants was a lumberman named McCartney of Red Rock, Charlotte County – "an observant and well-informed man" – who cut timber there around 1870. Reportedly, the creature had made deep furrows in the sand bordering the lake. James Woodbury claimed to have seen a slithery trail of slime left by the sea serpent making its way back and forth between the Bay of Fundy and Lake Utopia.

The lumbermen described it variously as having the head of an alligator and the head of a horse. But they generally agreed that the front section they saw was at least forty feet long. Several remarked on its frolicsome habit of suddenly making the still waters foam into froth and sending up showers of logs and spruce edgings into the surprised air.

Robert White was in charge of a crew bringing a raft of logs down the lake on a day when the mood hit the monster. Heavy logs flew up in all directions, and a "shining coil" arose in the middle of the raft only to disappear again as quickly. All the workers saw it.

Joseph Goodill claimed he watched the sea serpent "for quite a while" sunning itself in an open space in the spring ice break-up.

Victor Cook asserted he mistook it for a motorboat, it was speeding so fast, then saw its head and neck rise out of the water at a distance of three hundred yards.

In the last century a big Maine fair at Portland beat the drums for a super-special sideshow attraction, "The Great Sea Serpent of Passamaquoddy." The huge denizen on display closely fitted the description of the Utopia monster. Had it strayed afar and fallen victim to foul play? Some Charlotte County people got worried – it was as if they had lost an old friend. But the next year there was another reassuring report of the monster rearing its fearsome head in the lake, and everyone was happy again.

Should any credence be placed in such reports? Dr. Carl Medcof, a research scientist at the St. Andrews Fisheries Biological Station, certainly thinks so:

These stories should never be scoffed at merely because no physical explanation has yet been found. Some of the reports you hear from Lake Utopia are very convincing and they come from people considered highly reputable. There must be a valid explanation. For instance, it has been determined that eels ball up in huge knots in Nova Scotia – such a mass of eels, or several of them, could give the appearance of a sea monster in Utopia.

But it will take a lot of scientific ingenuity to explain away all the unnatural and seemingly supernatural phenomena that overflow New Brunswick's historical lore. While politicians argue over whether the province has lost population because of unemployed persons leaving, there's no doubt that our large population of resident spirits has been well maintained; they're staying in their old haunts.

We have silent ghosts, and ghosts that lift your scalp with eerie rising screams. We have invisible ghosts, and ghosts that appear as pirates wearing silver buckles, or, a favourite posture, with their heads tucked under their arms; or manifest themselves merely as dancing lights or flickering masses of flame at sea. Our fraternity of famous ghosts, with an encouraging absence of discrimination, includes equal numbers of Englishmen and Frenchmen and Indians, but especially young lovers. We even have a haunted mountain, and an island that became a ghost.

Silence emphatically is the rule on Isle Haute, out in the Bay of Fundy between New Brunswick and Nova Scotia. There, if you're lucky enough to dig in the exact right spot at midnight – the one midnight in seven years when the island shifts position – and if you utter not a sound, you will soon hear your shovel clang on Captain Kidd's treasure chest. The only trouble is, it's hard not to disqualify yourself by gasping aloud when a dazzling ball of light emanates from the hole and a headless buccaneer walks about in circles, mutely guarding the hoard.

A young St. Martins farmer, Charles Enfield, is reported to have rowed to Isle Haute to dig with a Micmac Indian. His anxious schoolmarm fiancée followed in another boat with her young brother. In a deafening thunderstorm at midnight, it is told, she overtook him and died in his arms in a blinding flash of light. He recovered consciousness only long enough to relate what happened; the Indian was never seen again; the young brother, espied the next morning on shore by a passing boat, never recovered his sanity.

So now there are more ghosts on Isle Haute.

Silence, however, is not the rule with the Dungarvon Whooper. This ghost's escalating scream, which freezes strong men in their tracks, pierces countless square miles of the storied Miramichi River timberland like a high-powered air-raid siren. It sounds like what legend says it is – the dying shriek of a nineteenth century lumbercamp cook having his throat cut in his sleep for his money belt. "With a rusty knife," someone once added, still quivering.

Most logical explanation: the wooing scream of the eastern panther, wily and elusive cousin of the Pacific mountain lion. Only a few are believed to exist in New Brunswick; for sixty years they were thought extinct. But scores of people have sighted them, and the Smithsonian Institute of Washington has definitely identified plaster casts of the big paw prints.

Another spectre that goes for the topless fad is the Penobsquis Pedlar – a travelling salesman murdered more than a century ago who on dark nights now travels with his head under his arm.

Undoubtedly the most exasperating spook ever, was the Firewood Man of Chatham. Night after night he kicked hardwood sticks around Earl Stevenson's basement, with resounding bangs and thumps that shook the house. But the spook never gave the Stevensons the satisfaction of showing their friends the evidence; he always had it neatly piled up again by next morning.

There are people in the Richibucto area of Kent County who swear they have seen the pirates with the silver buckles – visitors strangely garbed in flat feather-adorned hats, tight breeches, and cloaks – rowing a silent boat ashore at night. They are the spirits of English freebooters whose damaged brig sought refuge in Richibucto harbour and was overwhelmed by Indians led by an Acadian Expulsion fugitive, Louis de Grass.

Once a Richibucto Micmac explained the significance to a stranger: every time the pirate captain appears, an Indian dies. Next day the Micmac, hauling up his lobster traps, toppled overboard and drowned.

A stranger-than-usual apparition was the ghost of Thomas Glasier's Paddy Hollow Camp on the St. John River. A beautiful girl had met her death at a nearby American-owned lumber settlement in the 1860's – murdered by an obsessed and thwarted suitor, who fled.

Later the countryside was alarmed by frequent reports of a ghost with a horrible blanched face, and eyes with fire shooting out of them – a ghost that stole food. Many lumberjacks were thunderstruck by the sight.

By chance years afterward someone stumbled on a cave neatly hidden by tree branches. Inside, on the floor, he found a corpse, with eyes staring wide, unkempt hair down to its waist . . . and close by, an old axe, a yellowed letter, a faded tintype of a lovely young woman – and a home-made mask of white birch bark with eye-openings rimmed by red flannel.

If frustrated lovers make the most appealing ghosts, New Brunswick is a land brimming over with sweet, painful nostalgia. At Lorneville on the Fundy coast you may some night be lucky enough to see a lovely maiden in bridal dress and a handsome young man in marine uniform taking form out of the mist at Ghost Rock. They stand arm in arm – Florence Atherton and her intended groom, Captain James Trevarton of the Brig Minerva. On his wedding day he vanished, murdered by a jealous first mate, William Davis; and when Florence learned the truth from a letter after Davis' death, she died of a broken heart.

The beautiful Cup Carrier of Albert County is the ghost of a girl who, abandoned by her fiancé, didn't wait to linger – she downed a quick cup of poison.

Near the Tantramar Marshes you can take your choice of ghosts. Mirrored in the Missiguash River you may see the smiling shade of Marguerite, beauteous daughter of Governor Michel le Neuf de la Vallière, who proudly re-named the river for her and then changed it back to the Indian name when he found out that she planned to marry a commoner and widower with six children, Louis le Gannes.

Or you may see the spirits of five Frenchmen who drowned while crossing to the English side in 1754 against the orders of the priest le Loutre . . . or the spirits of the five English soldiers who were ambushed at Bloody Bridge, or the nine Indians they cut down in the fight to the death. (The road was eventually shifted and a new bridge built because local residents refused to use the haunted old one.)

Or near the Aulac stream you may meet the shadows of a young lieutenant and his girl friend who were captured and sentenced to death by the Micmacs in reprisal for the killing of some tribesmen by English troops. Both were tied to stakes on the mud flats, facing the incoming tide. The rising waters rippled over the man's head first, as he was nearer the river . . . and just then a group of Frenchmen arrived and saved the girl. But in desperation she plunged back into the river to join her lover in death.

However, the spectre you have the best chance of encountering in New Brunswick – and also the most eye-filling – is the burning Phantom Ship of Bay Chaleur. Admittedly it's a rare sight – nevertheless, over the years, hundreds of North Shore residents have glimpsed the fiery mass moving along the bay at night, flaring and fading at intervals and many have watched it for an hour or more. Usually it seems to portend a northwest storm.

Some swear it is the reincarnation of a square-rigged ship with tall masts; that amidst the leaping red flames you can see tiny black figures wriggling up the spars and running frantically around the deck.

To most, however, it is simply a huge, travelling, seething fire – "about as big as a house," said Frank Hornibrook of Stonehaven, "and I would guess ten to twelve miles out in the bay." The bay here is thirty miles across to Quebec's Gaspé shore.

Mr. Hornibrook is one of the luckier ones – he saw the phenomenon twice in two evenings. On a Sunday night, driving along the coast toward Bathurst, he viewed it for five minutes. Next evening he was visiting a neighbour, William Smith, and telling him about it when Mrs. Smith called out: "Look from this window quick. Your Phantom Ship is back again!" This time they watched it glide along for sixteen minutes before the apparition faded out.

Another neighbour, Bert Wood, was a confirmed skeptic. He comments, "I laughed for six months at Frank

Hornibrook when he said he saw the Phantom Ship ten years ago. Then one windy, rainy evening in September, 1969, the night Hurricane Gerda was to arrive, there it was out our window – as big as life and lit up so brilliantly from stem to stern, or end to end or whatever. And the speed of the thing – fantastic! In a half-hour it travelled thirty miles."

What is the Phantom Ship? A mirage? Not when all members of a family and their neighbours see the same thing; yet once, when several Shippegan Island fishermen tried to row out to it they discovered it was always about the same distance away from their cod boats. Is it a phosphorescent light or other chemicals or minerals? Is it the spectre of a ship storm-wrecked at Green's Point three centuries ago, as the superstitious suggest? Or – the Shippegan version – is it the ship's lantern from another ill-starred vessel, the *John Craig*, swinging in the sky?

Just as vivid, but a less frequent manifestation, is the burning ship of the Bay of Fundy off southern New Brunswick. Mrs. Horace Gillmor of Sussex recalls, "I saw it as a young girl, when a man sent his daughter over to our house to alert us. It certainly looked like a vessel enveloped in flames, and could not have been more than two miles out. We watched it for at least ten minutes."

The haunted mountain? That's up in the Tobique River country – known variously as the Burning Mountain and the Rumbling Mountain. For some reason the ground seems warmer there, grassy slopes turn green early, dead leaves dry up fast, and hikers, since anyone can remember, have said they hear groans and grumbles from under their feet. A sleeping volcano, perhaps; or just subterranean indigestion.

And the island that became a ghost? You can see it from Grand Manan in the Bay of Fundy – Inner Wood Island, a mile off shore. Settled many years ago because it was close to good fishing grounds, the island had a population of 120, including forty-one schoolchildren.

But passing time left Inner Wood Island behind. With modern diesel fishing craft, it was no longer essential to live with the fish. Phones and electricity could not be easily spun out to the little island. Wives complained, and daughters complained even more loudly.

It was a melancholy day for L. K. Ingersoll, District

School Supervisor, when he stepped off a fishing boat there one day in 1957 to close the school. By then only one family was left, and they were leaving too.

Today, deserted and lifeless, it is an unworldly place to visit. About fifteen homes still stand, some sagging, some with doors flapping, some with sightless eyes where once glass windows were. Only the creaking of loose doors breaks the heavy silence.

The old schoolhouse is now used only by cattle – placed out to graze on the island from early spring until late autumn – they evidently appreciate someone's foresight in building them a shelter from storms.

Still neat-looking is the little white Reformed Baptist Church with its white steeple, and across the road is a modest cemetery in a clearing, with the sea on one side.

You can walk into the church, up the aisle, past all the pews still in place, to the pulpit at the back with the Scripture reposing on it, open–just as though the clergy-man had stepped out for a moment to look and see if anyone was coming.

3 A Place of Many Meanings

Talk about the big colony of American draft dodgers in Toronto! Why, so many fugitives from military service swarmed over the Maine border into New Brunswick that the Mapleton district in Carleton County became known as "Skedaddle Ridge." But this wasn't in the Vietnam war; it was the American Civil War.

That's one of the most striking things about delving a bit into history – so little really has changed.

There was quite a controversy on about short hair or long hair for young men in June, 1794, when the Duke of Kent, father of the future Queen Victoria, visited Saint John. The dudes of the city, noticing he wore his coat collar up high, jumped to the conclusion that he wore his hair short and betook themselves to the barber to have their flowing locks trimmed. Next day they were crestfallen to discover the duke had long tresses.

Inflation was worrying pioneer shipbuilders at Saint John in 1800. A few years before, when James Simonds and James White had the first schooner, *Betsy*, built in 1769 to carry lumber, lime and fish to Boston and New-buryport, the cost worked out at twenty-three shillings fourpence a ton. By 1800 it was five pounds ten shillings a ton. Where would it all end?

Depressions came and went in those days too. During the slack year of 1819 a Saint John yard launched a ship called the *Hard Times*.

Prohibition is old stuff. At the instigation of teetotaller Hon. S. L. Tilley, a majority in the House of Assembly voted in 1855 to ban all alcoholic drinks – this in a convivial province where Jamaica rum had a been household staple since pioneer days, when it sold for eightpence a pint. It was well-known at that time that liquor gave men extra strength for hard physical labour. In ten and a half months in 1786, for a population of 20,000 people, 97,990 gallons of rum were imported along with much snuff but little tobacco (and little tea, which was a luxury). Many members of the House voted for prohibition as an astute political move, knowing the Legislative Council would throw the bill out anyway. The council didn't. Hundreds of tavern owners—more than two hundred in Saint John and Portland alone—faced ruin. The law, widely ignored, precipitated an election and was repealed within months.

Rising postal rates were ruffling tempers in the 1840's, when it cost sevenpence to send a letter from Saint John to Fredericton, a shilling to Richibucto, a shilling eightpence to Montreal. A copy of the laws of Prince Edward Island, mailed from Charlottetown to Fredericton at the request of the New Brunswick government, was billed a postal charge of £34 16s 8d; the province refused to call for it. Many nettled people preferred to send letters in the care of travelling friends.

As for our new international traffic signs in pictorial form, geologist Dr. Abraham Gesner found the same idea in the New Brunswick woods in the 1840's. His party of three white men and three Indians was unable to locate the old Indian portage between the St. Croix River headwaters and Eel River Lake – until they espied a drawing fastened to an old cedar tree. It was of a brave toting his canoe on his head. Later, when their lives were in danger as they neared a cataract in descending the Eel River, they saw a warning sketched in black on a wide piece of cedar fixed to a post – a picture of two Indians with heels uppermost behind a swamped canoe.

Inter-church co-operation – ecumenism – is "in" today. But Rev. Thomas Wood of New Jersey, back in 1753, became a Church of England missionary in Nova Scotia, struck up a lasting friendship with Abbé Maillard, Roman Catholic missionary to the Indians and Acadians, and the Abbé's papers enabled Wood to learn the Micmac language. In 1769 he toured the St. John River – the first Anglican cleric to arrive – and at Saint John one Sunday preached to the English in the morning, and, in their own tongues, to the Indians in the afternoon and the Acadian dyke-builders in the evening.

Conservation and pollution? Captain John Robb, R.N., of His Majesty's sloop *Satellite*, reporting in 1850 on his patrols in the Bay of Fundy, expressed grave misgivings for the future fisheries because Grand Manan fishermen caught so many tons of unwanted baby herring in their weirs and used them for field manure. He also deplored the habit of dumping fish offal (waste) on shore for the tide to carry back to the sea, which he thought would eventually contaminate the commercial fisheries.

Important social advances were being made, as now, every year. In the early 1800's the Legislative Assembly decided, purely in the interests of humanity, to transfer lunatics from their current place of incarceration, the Saint John Gaol, to the Almshouse.

And the younger generation? The outlook seemed hopeless in 1862. The Saint John *Weekly Telegraph* solemnly reported Justice Ritchie's allusion to a case of a young vagabond, whose parents paid him not the slightest attention, who, with his companions of fourteen and fifteen, was in the habit of sleeping in barns and shanties with "abandoned females of what age, think you? Not over fourteen years old! . . . a burning disgrace to a civilized people. . . . The experience of this Province, England and the United States shows that crime is largely on the increase. . . ."

And you can't help being awestruck, looking back into history, to see how very real and very earnest life was in the early days.

It was considered nothing at all for the French and English pioneers to cross the rolling ice-cold swells of the temperamental Bay of Fundy to Nova Scotia when emergency demanded. Partners of the pre-Loyalist Hazen-Simonds-White trading house at Saint John paddled, rowed or sailed across the bay several times when threatened by Indian uprisings or American rebel privateers, like the improbably named Captain A. Greene Crabtree. Louise, widow of the Sieur de Freneuse of Oromocto, once crossed in mid-winter with only an Indian paddler and her small son as companions. She had become involved in a scandal with the naval commandant at Port Royal, Captain St. Pierre Bonaventure, who persistently denied being implicated.

Unaccustomed harsh elements took a continual toll among early missionaries from France. In 1623 one of the first Recollets, Father Bernardian, died of hunger and exposure while walking through the forests from Miscou and Nepisiguit to the River St. John, where the missionaries were based.

The early English, so we're told, had an easier time than the earlier French. But it would be hard to persuade Mrs. Dorothy Kendrick to agree. At Gagetown in 1769, Rev. Thomas Wood baptized Joseph and Mary, twin children of John and Dorothy Kendrick. The clergyman wrote afterward, without further explanation, that the twins were born in an open canoe, two leagues from any house. Not in a canoe pulled up on a beach – an open canoe *on the St. John River*. Apart from everything else, it must have been quite a balancing act.

People took for granted then that it was a feat just to be born and to survive. Any woman who brought up a family of ten or twelve without losing any was so remarkable as to draw admiring, and oft-times envious, comments. You can see it on the Loyalist gravestones – so many commemorate babies, children, youths, young mothers.

By long experience, the Acadians were more adaptable than the novice pioneers from New England. Archdeacon Raymond's writings mention Michael Vienneau and his wife Thérèse, who lived in Maugerville and Memramcook. He died first, aged one hundred, she at ninety-six, their son in Pokemouche at 112, his son in Rogersville at ninety-six – a family record of 404 years.

Both Acadians and English married young. None of the pre-Loyalist New England settlers who founded the trading post that was to become Saint John married anyone beyond seventeen. James Simonds wed Hannah Peabody, sixteen; James White wed her sister Elizabeth, seventeen; Jonathan Leavitt wed a third sister, Hephrabeth, sixteen. And William Hazen wed Sarah LeBaron, fifteen. Not surprisingly, early marriages often led to big broods. Judge Edward Winslow wrote to a friend in Halifax on January 17, 1793:

My two annual comforts, a child and a fit of the gout, return invariably. They came together this heat and, as

Forrest used to say, made me as happy as if the Devil had me. The boy is a fine fellow – of course – and makes up the number nine now living. My old friend Mrs. Hazen at the same time produced her nineteenth.

In 1786, when the seat of provincial government was moved from Saint John, you still couldn't travel to and from Fredericton except through the forest or by the St. John River and other waterways. So when Governor Thomas Carleton heard in March, 1788, that his brother, Lord Dorchester, Governor of British North America, was ill in Quebec, to get to his bedside he had no choice but to follow the couriers' route.

During spring freshets, when the waters were rushing down, Indians had paddled from Quebec all the way to Saint John and Port Royal in four days. For Governor Thomas Carleton the mid-winter trip on snowshoes from Fredericton – nearly four hundred miles – took nine days, including eight nights under canvas on the trail.

But the governor enjoyed a luxury excursion compared with pioneer travellers from New Brunswick to Prince Edward Island in the winter. They had a choice. They could pay $4 and just sit passively, wearing their safety harness, in the eighteen-foot open skiff, while it was rowed with steel-tipped oars through the sludge ice of nine-mile-wide Northumberland Strait, and alternately hauled over ice pans – or they could pay only $2 and get out and help pull the double-keeled craft, like a double-runner sled, across the ice. Many a passenger took an economy seat, because using his safety harness as a workhorse harness gave him a chance to warm up during one of the coldest ferry voyages known to man.

Yes, life could be very primitive and cruel, even in the last century. During the 1847 Irish potato famine, more than two thousand of the gaunt, emaciated immigrants en route to Saint John – jampacked into unsanitary plague-ridden "fever ships" – never even enjoyed a taste of the new life they so often dreamed of. Eight hundred typhus victims were buried at sea; six hundred more were buried on Partridge Island at the entrance to the harbour, where the quarantine station was. Toward the end of the epidemic, when all the doctors were laid low and bodies were beginning to pile up in the "dead-house," many were lowered into a common grave-trench on the island, and there, for the next century, the grass grew greener than anywhere else. Still another six hundred died in the Saint John Poor House hospital and were interred on the mainland. Celtic crosses on the island and ashore honour their memory.

Seemingly miraculously, the young city of Saint John, which had been braced for an epidemic, was not badly stricken itself. But this proved to be a brief respite. Just one lone ship, the *Blanche*, in 1854 brought the spark that touched off disaster: a case of Asiatic cholera which had been spreading to the West.

In the ghastly summer that ensued, people collapsed on all sides, too fast for the grave-diggers to keep up. The season's toll: 1,500 deaths in the Saint John-Portland population of fewer than 30,000 – one person in every twenty.

For sheer, protracted strain, it would be hard to eclipse the nightmare journey of Gamaliel Smethurst in 1761. It covered only the distance from Bathurst along Bay Chaleur and down the east coast to Fort Cumberland (Beausejour) – a trip a motorist today would make in a leisurely four or five hours. Smethurst had arrived at Bathurst aboard his brigantine in late October, the first English-speaking trader to visit the Nepisiguit area, with glittering hopes of a bonanza in trading with the Acadians and Micmacs for furs. They welcomed him enthusiastically.

Just as he was saying farewell, a British warship came in sight. It carried Captain MacKenzie and fifty Highlanders from Fort Cumberland. Their mission: seize and deport all Acadians, because French privateers from some unknown base had been harassing British ships. In vain did Smethurst plead that these were innocent and humble folk. Then he saw the 180 French captives and their Indian allies glaring at him, and heard the remarks spat in his direction, and he realized they thought he had been a decoy for a British trap.

Words would avail nothing. All he could do was get out. And then – to his horror – he was left behind.

Smethurst's ship, aground on a sandbar, was refloated by wind and tide while he was ashore looking for a lighter to unload the vessel. The already unnerved captain was panic-stricken to hear Indian war parties were on their way from the Restigouche area (now Campbellton) to avenge the round-up of the Acadians. He hoisted anchor and sailed away.

For two days the trader hid in a deserted Acadian hovel; he recalled in his memoirs that he "durst not make a fire for fear of discovery," as there were French and Indians on the other side of the bay. To ease his hunger pangs he caught a few ortolans – a bird resembling the junco or snowbird. But finally he had to throw himself upon the mercy of the remaining inhabitants.

With loud cohoops the Indians leaped on him, pinioned his arms; then they took him to the Acadians, offering to despatch him after appropriate torture.

Arguing desperately for his life, Smethurst managed to convince the French that he was blameless. And so, travelling by canoe or skiff, with the help of French or Indian guides, for the next six weeks he pursued an intermittent, wearying and often painful journey home. Almost everywhere he had to deny to the Indians that he had conspired in the abduction of the Acadians. Of the Micmac council at Pookmoosh (Pokemouche) he wrote later: "They said the English were a very cunning people, for I had been pretending to trade with the French at Nepisiguit, and had collected them together, and the English came with a net and catched them all."

Often his voyage was interrupted by violent storms, lasting for days – once he was on the verge of starvation, his rations reduced to the skin of one fish – and further delayed by hunting forays of whatever settlement he was in. On November 20 he wrote, "The Frenchman where I lodged, and most of the village, set off this morning for Port Miscou to hunt sea-cows (walrus) for their oil, which they make use of in the winter instead of butter."

At the Miramichi River, November 18, Smethurst had to be carried from his canoe to a hut – his legs numbed from six hours of cramped sitting in a bark canoe, soaking in frigid salt water up to his waist. There he was befriended by an Acadian named Beausoliel, who brought him flour and rum – ironically, a gesture of generosity to an Englishman from a Frenchman who had been expelled to Carolina but wended his way back again via the Mississippi.

The wreck of an English cargo vessel in a Miramichi

Bay storm brought Smethurst his most harrowing experience – the Indians got into the ship's eighty puncheons of brandy, and later, aflame with liquor, menaced him with muskets at a council in a wigwam. Their resentment against the English air of superiority vented itself repeatedly – one brave angrily said in French he was as great a man as the governor of Halifax, then pointed to his chief and added in English, "All one, King George."

But also the wreck brought the exhausted trader an unexpected windfall – a bundle of a year's issues of English newspapers, some very fresh and timely, hardly more than a month old, and, after they dried out, Smethurst forgot his aches and anxieties as he caught up intently with the tidings of his friends – some now dead, some married, some enriched, some bankrupt.

On December 9 he came to a large river called Chedaic (Shediac) full of loose ice, where "a sea-cow lifted its head out of the water, and came swimming after the canoe. A Frenchman soon shot it. It had two large teeth out of the water in the upper jaw pointing downward – these serve for defence, to climb rocks with, & c. A full-grown sea-cow will make two barrels of oil in autumn, when they are fattest. They are easily killed with a ball – very unwieldy – much like Anson's sea lions.* The French use the oil of these creatures to their meat – it is to me as rank as seal oil. ... The most noted places for their present resort are the islands of Magdelines and Point Miscou, but the sea-cows, wildfowl, Indians and beaver will leave us as we settle in the country, and go to places less frequented."

Apparently Smethurst was hardened enough to withstand the worst rigours by the time December arrived. His diary tells of being forced to walk along the shore, crawling under branches and often breaking through the ice, as the sea was too turbulent and the canoe too loaded – and of wading one icy stream, chest-deep, carrying his beaver coat on his head and his memorandum book in his mouth. It was after sunset on December 12 that he staggered into an English home at Baie Verte; still in his pocket were dried strips of Indian dog, the emergency food reserve.

Little-known exploits like Gamaliel Smethurst's remind us New Brunswick teems with history – history that belongs to all of Canada – for this is where the action was,

*Sea elephants

this is where men fought and died in ceaseless struggles with each other and with the elements, while the prairies still slumbered peacefully on, awaiting the creak and rumble of the westward wagons.

So plentiful are these bygone events that sometimes they jostle each other, trying to find elbow-room in one spot. Look at the stratified history found in layers at Portland Point in Saint John harbour:

(1) "Red Paint" Indian burial ground dating back 3,500 to 4,000 years; in the bottom of each grave is a covering of red ochre, bright red oxide scraped off rocks.

(2) Micmac Indian campsites of the Middle Ages.

(3) Fort La Tour, 1630-1645, the storied stronghold fiercely defended by erstwhile actress, Madame La Tour.

(4) A later French settlement, 1685-1696, believed to have been built by French Governor de Villebon.

(5) "Modern" Indian graves between 1696 and 1762 (these are above the Villebon settlement level, and contain French trading goods).

(6) Hazen, Simonds and White trading post, 1762 and after, preceding the Loyalists' arrival – a post operated by New Englanders who stood by Britain in the American Revolutionary War and helped prevent Maine from swallowing up New Brunswick.

(7) Also traces of subsequent wooden shipbuilding, a nail factory, a coal yard.

This has been one of Canada's richest storehouses of artifacts – Indian pottery, French cannon, dishes made in Newburyport, Massachusetts, in the 1770's, to mention only a few items.

Perhaps because New Brunswick has been so abundantly lavished with historical landmarks, it is only lately that they are becoming truly appreciated and individually spotlighted. Not until 1961, for instance, was "Jenny's Well" – the site of English reformer, William Cobbett's, romance – rediscovered in Saint John. Not until 1969 was it brought to light that the tower clock in Fredericton's Christ Church Cathedral – built in 1853 as the first Cathedral foundation on English soil since the Norman Conquest – is an older brother of Big Ben, and was probably a tryout for Westminster's famed timepiece. Both were designed by Sir Edmund Beckett Denison, later Lord Grimthorpe, and in both the pendulum regulates the time-keeping of the clock through an invention of his known as the "gravity escapement." And not until 1970 was the first step toward the development of the Fort La Tour historical complex announced.

Meanwhile, on the St. John River twenty miles above Fredericton, at Prince William a realistic 1867 village has taken form – New Brunswick's biggest single historical project – at a cost of several millions. Old dwellings from the Mactaquac hydro-electric dam headpond area have been grouped on a three-hundred-acre site as the restored living settlement of "King's Landing," with church, school, store, agricultural hall, complete with authentic touches from obsolete harrows to rustic snake fences.

The next biggest venture – but potentially more important – is the continuing underwater quest for what remains from the Battle of the Restigouche, the 1760 naval clash in which Commodore "Foul Weather" Jack Byron, grandfather of the poet, crushed a weaker French force after a long-drawn-out siege and thus demolished France's last stand in North America.

Already a massive ten-foot cannon weighing several tons, retrieved from the French frigate *Le Marchault*, is on display in a Campbellton park. A full-scale exhibition of relics of this climactic battle could become a major Canadian historical attraction on New Brunswick's North Shore.

But history is everywhere in New Brunswick. You find it around every sweeping turn of the St. John River. Practically every headland once contained a fort or at least an early mansion. For example, little Caton's Island in the Long Reach – here, on "Isle Emenic," was established as New Brunswick's first permanent European settlement around 1610. And here Father Biard celebrated mass – the first recorded religious observance in the province.

Farther up river is Jemseg (Great Marshes), from which the little Jemseg River leads to expansive Grand Lake. Here Colonel Thomas Temple, named governor by Cromwell in 1657, erected a fort – the first outpost built by the English on the St. John River. Then, in succession, a new treaty in Europe ousted Temple and the English; the French took over; the fort was captured by the Dutch and Acadia was re-named New Holland; a Boston force drove out the Dutch; the French regained possession and things were back to normal.

De Villebon re-built Jemseg fortress in 1690, but abandoned it two years later to construct a more formidable stronghold at Nachouac (Nashwaak) opposite Fredericton.

From here he masterminded the savage hammer-blows by French-led Maliseets, Micmacs, Passamaquoddies and Penobscots against New England villages. These unceasing massacres prompted Lieutenant-Governor William Stoughton of Massachusetts to instruct Acadian-hunter, Major Benjamin Church, to organize an expedition to eradicate that fester-point – "on the St. John's River in Nova Scotia" – which he described in his letter as "the chief source from whence the most of our disasters do issue."

In the meantime Jemseg had become the peaceful estate of Louis d'Amours, the Sieur de Chauffours, and his wife Marguerite, the couple who opened up a new life for the Indians' slave-boy, John Gyles.

It was at Nachouac that Chevalier Robineau de Villebon, in an excess of patriotic zeal as he fired up the Indians' enthusiasm for another great foray against New England, made Chief Taxous his blood brother, presented him with his gilt-trimmed officer's coat, tossed a hatchet up in the air and skillfully caught it, then did a spasmodic tribal war dance, trembling, shaking and wailing like a wolf.

Speaking of governors and dances – in the more tranquil era of the mid-1800s Governor Manners-Sutton at Fredericton made history of a sort. At Christmas he ordered his officers to dance a polka quadrille for the Indians, who smoked their pipes with satisfaction and watched. The governor's reasoning: "As the Indians were good enough to dance all the rest of the year for you, you should be good enough to dance for the Indians at Christmas." There is no record of the officers' reaction.

An unusual historical personality was Charles des Champs de Boishébert, the French officer whom Monckton drove from the St. John River in 1758. With great resourcefulness Boishébert stage-managed the exodus of about 3,500 Acadians from their settlements to the deep woods before the British could capture and exile them – sometimes snatching them from under the very noses of the advancing troops. He was an inveterate optimist, and buoyantly helped keep their spirits up. Yet capricious fate was unfair to him. Even "Boishébert's Island" in the Miramichi, where a town of refugees sprang up, lost its identification with him; it has been corrupted to Beaubear's Island, the name of another settler. And Boishébert himself, returning to France after the cession to Britain, was imprisoned in the Bastille as a suspected accomplice in the machinations of Bigot, the infamous Intendant of Quebec. It was fifteen months before he was cleared and freed.

But the most anguished moment of Boishébert's life – the moment any of his countrymen would have dreaded – was that instant in the early morning of September 13, 1759, when he happened to glance out the window of his Quebec hospital room and became the first Frenchman to see the British forces drawn up for battle on the Plains of Abraham. Instantly he raised the alarm, and General Montcalm on his hasty arrival commented bitterly: "There they are, just where they ought not to be!"

It's doubtful whether Boishébert, at the worst of times, considered himself as misfortune-prone as Nicholas Denys, governor of the Gulf of St. Lawrence from Canso to Gaspé in the middle 1600's. Bathurst's first white settler, Denys lived chiefly at Pointe au Père (Ferguson Point) and often seemed to have everything going his way. But just as often he ran into the same road-block as Charles de La Tour – the consuming obsession of d'Aulnay Charnisay to be the unchallenged ruler of Acadia.

Both Denys and Charnisay had come out to North America in 1632 as lieutenants of Governor de Razilly. It was not long before young Denys built up a flourishing timber trade, using de Razilly's ships. Then de Razilly died, and the sky fell in on Denys. His rival, Charnisay, became the new governor, cut off his timber exports and later drove him out of Miscou. Charnisay drowned in 1650 – but his widow kept up the persecution, seizing Denys' trading posts and having him borne off in irons to a dungeon in Quebec on a framed charge.

After some months he was released, and returned to Bathurst to set up trading outposts and forts in Acadia under a commission from the Company of New France. But now Le Borgne, claiming to be Charnisay's successor, ambushed and imprisoned him and put the torch to his properties. When freed, Denys returned to Paris, got a new commission backed by the King, happily came back and built anew in Cape Breton – and then, when a flash-fire broke out, literally lost everything but his shirt . . . "All my people were forced to flee the fire's violence entirely naked, in shirts only."

Nevertheless this extremely persevering pioneer came back to Bathurst, wrote a book about Acadia, and went to France to have it published. The returns were negligible. In 1685, withered and sere, he existed in Paris in beggary.

And yet guess who appeared again in Bathurst the very next year, a frail bent old man of eighty-eight years, as full of ambition as ever? But by now Nicholas Denys was no longer a great adventurer but just another settler. No one knows where his grave was dug; but a cairn in Bathurst honours the notable historical figure.

Ironically, the greatest mistake Nicholas Denys made in his storm-tossed life was to consider himself a failure. For though he left no material riches, this fur trader, fisherman and naturalist bequeathed to posterity *A Geographical and Historical Description of the Coasts of North America*, a comprehensive work beyond price.

It's not hard to see, from his writings, why Cocagne on the East coast was one of Denys' favourite spots. Its name means "place of plenty," and he tells why:

All my people were so surfeited with game and fish that they wished no more, whether wild geese, ducks, teal, plover, snipe large and small, pigeons, hares, partridges, young partridges, salmon, trout, mackerel, smelt, oysters and other kinds of good fish. All I can tell you is this, that our dogs lay beside the meat and fish, so much were they satisfied with it.

Such history New Brunswick is bringing back to life in a growing number of museums, rehabilitated homesteads and other landmarks. Some structures have been restored with almost unbelievable painstaking. Salvaged from its former use as a barn, an 1833 Carleton County building at Upper Woodstock – a pioneer county courthouse in New Brunswick – is today a showplace of historical fidelity. Its plaster is made of flaked lime, sand and cow's hair. The window panes are from buildings of the time; so are the square nails. The barristers' quarters have a mahogany washstand, ewer and basin, home-made soap and linen towels woven from flax.

You'll find others now almost everywhere you look ... Acadian museums at the University of Moncton and at Caraquet, Chaleur Area Historical Museum at Dalhousie, Miramichi Natural History Museum at Chatham, Westmorland Centennial Museum (Keillor House) at Dorchester, Richibucto River Historical Society Museum at Richibucto, St. Louis College Museum at Edmundston, Royal Canadian Dragoons Museum at Camp Gagetown, Sir Leonard Tilley House at Gagetown, Kings County Museum at Hampton, Albert County Museum at Hopewell Cape, Civic Historical Collection at Hartland, Campobello Library Association at Welchpool, Roosevelt Campobello Cottage and International Park, Grand Manan Museum at Grand Harbor, 1812 Blockhouse at St. Andrews, Fort Beauséjour Museum at Aulac.

In Saint John are the New Brunswick Museum, Martello Tower, Loyalist House, Georgian Courthouse and spiral stairway, old general store, barber shop and one-room schoolhouse. Fredericton has its York-Sunbury Museum in the old Officers' Quarters, the venerable Arts Building – oldest college building in Canada – at the University of New Brunswick, which now operates in conjunction with St. Thomas University. And in the Legislative Library, handled by attendants with white-glove care, is the world's most perfect set of John James Audubon's volumes "Birds Of America," with their huge hand-tinted illustrations. In the Moncton area, if you feel optimistic, you can dig for buried treasure – nine bags of French army pay gold – in suburban Irishtown, or even gigantic mastodon bones in nearby Hillsborough. And here in the Hub city is the old Free Meeting House, an extraordinary centre, used as a place of worship by twelve faiths for nearly a century and a half.

But besides being, mile for mile, one of Canada's richest historical lodes, New Brunswick is many other things – a land of many meanings for many people, and this may account for the strong pull the old province still exerts on those who have packed up and left for distant fields where the greenbacks grow thicker.

It is, as the tourist pamphlets say, the Picture Province – so plentifully endowed with lakes and rivers that from the air it sometimes seems the land is a cluster of islands. No home in New Brunswick is farther than ten miles from open countryside. Workers can be spinning a line for their first trout, or taking aim at their first duck, while their cousins in Montreal or Toronto are still inching through urban traffic.

It's also the Forest Province – leaning more heavily on the timberlands than any other province. It has emerged from the epoch of uncountable sawmills and the huge long-timber stream drives into the era of pulp and paper mills, motorized transportation, planned reforestation, full exploitation of the entire tree, softwood and hardwood alike. Everything today is streamlined, mechanized, computer-ized, cost-accounted. Gone are the old leisurely days when stiff-collared exporters sent lumber shipments overseas almost as a matter of course – when one Saint John dealer could count on loading four full cargoes of timber yearly for London to be made into school slate-frames for the Empire.

And it's the River Province – a great distinction many New Brunswickers grow up almost unaware of, because they assume lordly rivers are natural wherever you live. No part of North America can compare in this respect. The breathtakingly scenic St. John River, the Rhine of America, is 450 miles long. There's the Miramichi River, the greatest Atlantic salmon sports network in the world, which, with its myriad tributaries, looks like a map of the nerve system of the human body.

Then there's the sparkling Restigouche with its cele-brated pools where wealthy American anglers and their flown-in guests have spent as much as $1,000 per salmon to bring home fish – indeed, sometimes $1,000 per pound of salmon. And there are the more precipitous Upsalquitch and the almost Swiss-like Sevogle, named after the Micmac word for cliffs, where you can feel chilly at eleven o'clock of a hot morning because the sun hasn't risen high enough yet to beam straight down on you between the rocky walls.

To some it's the United Empire Loyalist Province, because the Loyalists gave New Brunswick its first mas-sive wave of settlement. To others it's the Acadian Pro-vince because this is where many Acadian descendants live.

In any event New Brunswick is a province born of two great migratory movements – two groups of displaced persons – the Loyalists and the Acadians. And it's an interesting fact that this little province is a unique "capsule of Canada" – for here the English-French population ratio, at sixty to forty, is nearest to that of the nation as a whole.

Surprisingly, the ratio was exactly the same before the Loyalists came. In 1783 the future province already contained 3,000 English and 2,000 French. But this does not mean the population was 5,000, as often cited, because that figure leaves out the 2,000 Indians. So there were 7,000 people – and the 14,000 Loyalists had the effect of tripling the population.

Besides Acadians, earlier arrivals than the Loyalists included the Yorkshire settlers in the Chignecto Isthmus area, Channel Islanders in the northeast, New Englanders around Maugerville, Burton, Gagetown, Sackville, Passamaquoddy and on the Petitcodiac River; a few Scottish fishermen on the Miramichi, Nepisiguit and Restigouche rivers; and six prolific German families from Pennsylvania who landed in 1763 on the bank of the Petitcodiac, from where their descendants spread – the Stieffs (Steeves), Trites, Lutz, Jonas (Jones), Rickers and Somers.

To landscape photographers New Brunswick is the Province of Covered Bridges. Though it has lost hundreds of these romantic spans to time and to burgeoning traffic in the last generation, it still possesses an extraordinary total of 146, which represents ten per cent of the covered bridges in the world. They include five of the ten longest "kissing bridges" anywhere – a term from horse-and-buggy days – and the granddaddy of them all, the 1,282-foot-long covered bridge over the St. John River at Hartland. They were enclosed, not to keep snow off the floor, as many people today imagine (in the old days snow had to be carried by the wagonload to be spread on the floor so sleighs could get through), but to retard the rotting of the timbers by weather. An open bridge was calculated good for ten years, a covered bridge for eighty.

It's also a province of picturesque names – many of them legacies from the Maliseet and Micmac tribes, and the Passamaquoddies who spoke a tongue very much like Maliseet. Tourists are startled, near a peaceful lake of the same name, to see a little rustic graveyard with this solemn inscription:

1800   1871

HA HA CEMETERY

Here lie the Remains

of

John Smith Esq.

Founder and First Representative

Of the County of Albert

These Indians were mostly migratory hunters, lean and lithe in contrast to the more sedentary physique of their New England Abeñaki cousins who raised corn and other crops. Their lightweight, birchbark canoes, compared with ponderous dugouts, had the swiftness of arrows. Their stamina awed the white men. In the 1860's a Maliseet, Louis Sappier, indignant when a stagecoach driver in Fredericton refused to accept him as a fare for the sixty-mile trip to Woodstock, retorted he'd get there on foot ahead of the stagecoach. And he did, staggering and careening only yards ahead, but ahead nevertheless. He collected a $5 bet from the driver.

Later Louis Sappier challenged the pioneer paddle-wheeler, *Reindeer*, sailing the St. John River over the same route. He was cheerily sitting on the wharf when the steamer chuffed up.

In the middle 1800's Richibucto exporter, L. W. Des-Brisay, had a Micmac runner named Jim who regularly trotted away at noon with mail for Chatham forty miles distant and was back the next morning.

If you've assumed that early Indians tended to be short, black-eyed and muscularly powerful, you may be surprised to find that geologist Dr. Abraham Gesner in 1847 reported the Maliseets and Micmacs as having the same hazel eyes, copper coloring, straight coarse black hair, high cheek bones, scanty beard, erect carriage, and "some of the men are upwards of six feet in height, and remarkable for suppleness, activity and great powers of endurance, rather than for strength."

He remarked they may travel seventy miles in a day under heavy burdens, without food and without apparent fatigue. "Bears, deer, moose and other animals are sometimes pursued by them and overtaken. The skill and agility they display in ascending and descending the dangerous rapids on many of the rivers, in their canoes, has never been attained by Europeans; and the quickness of their perceptions in discovering the trails and footsteps, and even the scents, of men and animals, is truly surprising."

But New Brunswick's role of greatest significance, perhaps, is as a Province of Peace – not only because the English and French inhabitants learned to live together, but because New Brunswickers and their neighbours on all sides have too.

Conflicts raged in and around us for centuries – French against French, French against English, British against Americans – and yet the province paradoxically stands out more as a unique haven of goodwill than as a battleground stained with blood.

All through its early history New Brunswick was tugged, wrenched and pushed every-which-way. It was part of Acadia; then it was renamed New Alexandria in 1624 by Sir William Alexander (and Nova Scotia was renamed New Caledonia). Saint John became Clinton in honour of Sir Henry Clinton, and the St. John River became the Clyde on English maps for more than a century. Meanwhile the province became temporarily New Holland; eventually it became part of Nova Scotia; and when a new name was sought, New Ireland was considered for a while, also Pittsylvania in tribute to William Pitt. Can you imagine living in Clinton, Ptt.?

Even the shape of Acadia was always in doubt, depending on which power legally possessed it. That power – England or France – claimed it extended to the Penobscot River in Maine. The other power claimed it denoted only the Nova Scotia peninsula.

New Brunswick ran into boundary disputes on all sides. The first governor, Col. Thomas Carleton, had to fight off a determined bid by Nova Scotia in 1803 to extend her boundaries by slicing off eastern New Brunswick all the way up to the head of tide in the Restigouche River. Then he had to contend with the determination of his brother, Sir Guy Carleton, Lord Dorchester, governor of British North America at Quebec, to appropriate Madawaska County. At Edmundston it is said the brothers conferred at St. Rose de Degalis, a village between that city and Rivière du Loup, and began rolling dice after dinner. The see-saw game went on all night – and at dawn Col. Thomas Carleton was one point ahead. He picked up Madawaska for New Brunswick.

Undoubtedly they did meet on common ground. One folk story says they were coming down the Restigouche together by canoe when a homesteader fired a shot across their bow. Musket in hand, he demanded papers to show he was entitled to his lot. He got them. His land, incidentally, included part of the later "Millionaires Pool" – which has changed hands several times among wealthy salmon anglers for fabulously soaring prices.

New Brunswick's trouble with Maine revolved on a question: Which river was the true Ste. Croix of Champlain and deMonts? The English wanted to place it as far westward as the Penobscot in Maine. The New Englanders claimed it was the Magaguadavic, which would lop off western New Brunswick as far as St. George, half-way from Calais to Saint John. It would have left the province with only 120 miles of the St. John River.

Tension on the border tightened until almost any small mis-step could have triggered a war. Bizarre happenings occurred. John Baker hoisted an American flag at Baker's Brook on the St. John, and Sheriff Miller of York County bravely, if reluctantly, marched himself over, arrested Baker in his bed and marched him back into jail at Fredericton. Near Fort Fairfield, opposing forces glared at each other across the St. John River. Folklore has it that red-headed Paddy McGarrigle, John Glasier's favourite cook, innocently crossed the river on a stroll with his mammoth girl friend – he in red pants and shirt, she in her red dress – and in effect captured the town, which they found deserted. The Yankees, Paddy always maintained, thought the whole redcoat army was coming.

That's the story of war in New Brunswick – lots of marching up and marching down, but few fatalities. Upwards of 100 battles have been tabulated, but the death list is under 200.

The Maliseets and Micmacs were ferociously warlike – but they inflicted their attacks on far-away New England.

The Fenian invasion of New Brunswick, much heralded, amounted to just a few skirmishes.

The 104th Regiment, which made its famous midwinter march from Fredericton to Quebec through the wilderness in twenty-four days without losing one of its six hundred soldiers to exposure, fought courageously through the War of 1812 – but far from New Brunswick soil.

(And it fought in old tattered and patched uniforms, for the new replacement tunics and trousers were captured when the privateer *Rover* of Salem, Massachusetts, seized the merchantman *Juniper* in the Bay of Fundy. The Americans were delighted to get the uniforms, as the United States market had no scarlet cloth. The American commissioner of purchases bought the 1,100 coats for $4 each – "red coats, white or buff collars, cuffs and tips, and handsomely ornamented." They were distributed to American bandsmen.)

Despite the fact that the English assault on Fort Beauséjour in the Chignecto area in June, 1755, was intended to be a full-scale effort, casualties were so negligible that it has gone down in history as "The Velvet Siege of Beauséjour." When an English shell exploded in a supposedly bomb-proof casement, killing three Frenchmen and an English prisoner, that settled it. The defenders surrendered and invited the English officers to a sumptuous dinner.

This was hardly a decisive strategic victory. England and France were always exchanging prizes around the negotiation table, and strongholds and land passed from one to the other more often by the stroke of a pen than the roar of a cannon. Even after the New Englanders in 1745 performed the phenomenal feat of capturing Fort Louisbourg, England didn't keep it. Whitehall said to France in effect: "Very well, let us have Madras and we'll let you have Louisbourg back."

Little wonder that Boston was infuriated with the British government.

But two battles that took place in New Brunswick did mark turning-points in Canadian history.

One was the thwarted attempt by Colonel Jonathan Eddy of Massachusetts, a renegade Nova Scotian, to seize Fort Cumberland (Beauséjour) during the American Revolutionary War. If the Hazen-Simonds-White partnership at Saint John had not kept the St. John River Indians from running amok, there seems no question that Fort Cumberland would have fallen and New Brunswick today might be part of Maine.

Colonel Eddy had a ragtag army of 180 New Englanders, Maugerville settlers, Cumberland farmers and some Indians – too few to do the job.

The other crucial encounter was the last naval clash of the Seven Years' War, the 1760 Battle of the Restigouche, fought near the modern site of Campbellton with such fury that for generations afterward the forests were pock-marked with cannonball wounds.

Had this French force been able to fight its way out of the Restigouche and break through the British blockade of the St. Lawrence to retake Quebec, it might have changed the entire history of North America.

By a curious twist of fate, Britain lost more men to brandy than to French guns in the Battle of the Restigouche. Six English sailors got into the liquor hold on a captured French stores ship and would not come out again, despite repeated shouts from their shipmates above that the vessel had been set afire. All six died.

As it was, the battle probably saved more lives than it cost, for the arriving French warships had found a large Acadian refugee settlement slowly starving to death, try-ing to subsist by chewing beaver skins. Wrote a French naval officer, Dangeac, in his diary: "I caused them each to be given half a pound of flour a day and one quarter of a pound of beef . . . . This little help rescued them from death's door."

But perhaps the most magnetic appeal of New Bruns-wick – both to visitors and to its wanderlust-stricken sons, returning as tourists – is its very diversity. Into a small package are crammed as many contrasts as several pro-vinces packed into one.

There are two climates – you can have your choice. Bake in the inland heat or sleep under blankets the year around on the coast beside Nature's great air-conditioner, the Bay of Fundy, the nemesis of tropical-suit manu-facturers.

Even sea-bathing comes in three varieties – balmy in the shallow waters of Northumberland Strait, cool off the un-crowded beaches of Bay Chaleur, exhilaratingly cold in Fundy.

Look at the contrasts – in the Tantramar Marsh country, lush hayfields, reclaimed from the sea, stretching to the horizon, dotted with lonely barns; in the west of New Brunswick, potatoes being grown the way the West grows grain, the "potato houses" looking like dwellings that have sunk so deep into the ground they now consist mainly of high-peaked roofs; the 427-square-mile battle manoeuvre area of Base Gagetown, Canada's largest combat training camp, which includes Canada's most minutely planned town, Oromocto. And the peat bogs of the North Shore, Shippegan and Miscou, where old folks can walk the spongey ground with a bounce they haven't possessed in fifty years; the red soil, reminiscent of Prince Edward Island, that distinguishes the summer resort town of St. Andrews-by-the-Sea, with its dignified mansions and house-and-garden tours and Art and Nature workshops and impressive Sir James Dunn Arena.

And the exciting, mineral-rich north, where mining companies have swarmed in to make Bathurst the fastest-growing city in the Atlantic area; the sharply-defined difference between New Brunswick's staid old buildings and the imposing architectural benefactions of Lord Beaverbrook, like The Playhouse in Fredericton and the Beaverbrook Gallery, which contains treasures intriguing not only for their cultural importance but in many cases for their news interest; the startling transformation in northeastern New Brunswick's fishing industry in a generation – once thousands of cod caught on hand-lines and set-lines were spread out on the shore, drying in the sun, to be shipped to Italy, Spain and the Caribbean as salted fish. Today thousands of residents of Caraquet and Shippegan work in modern fish-processing factories, factories kept supplied by Canada's biggest concentration of dragger-type vessels, or mini-trawlers.

And the fascinating, forested Miramichi country with its annual festival of folk songs which are apt to dwell on catastrophes like the explosive Great Miramichi Fire of 1825–ballads sung in a traditional old five-note scale that sounds as exotic to unaccustomed ears as Javanese music. Many of the tunes go back to the Crusades. Hundreds of such ballads exist; historian Dr. Louise Manny went out to the timberlands and recorded many of them for the Beaverbrook collection.

And the "Republic of Madawaska," the most individualistic county, the most bilingual part of the province. Groups of school-children romping along the street may be talking English one moment, French the next, like leaves blown this way or that by an unpredictable breeze. Here are blended four influences – Acadian, English, New England and Quebec – and the result is a lively, uninhibited, fun-loving region that belies New Brunswick's reputation as a cautious place where people when asked "How are you today?" don't say "Great!" but instead, after due thought, "Not bad."

The French Madawaskañs are sometimes called the "Brayons," a term derived from their ancestors who grew lin for linseed and for cloth-straw, and sometimes are fondly nicknamed the "Pancakes," while they call their Quebec neighbours the "Cañayen," or the "Blueberries." Citizens of the Republic of Madawaska have their own coat-of-arms, featuring a handclasp, and their own flag with an eagle and six stars.

Even the three principal cities are completely different. Saint John is in one sense still a Loyalist town with its King Square in the shape of the old Union Flag, and the Royal coat-of-arms of the Commonwealth of Massachusetts in nearby Trinity Church. But it is also Canada's most extensively planned and re-developed city, with many new facilities, such as a University of New Brunswick branch, and it is looking to tremendous growth in the next decade to double its size.

Hearty, aggressive Moncton is the most "Western" city in the Maritimes – some think of it as an American city – historically a railway and distribution centre and expecting to be some day the largest city in the Atlantic area and perhaps the capital of a united regional province.

Fredericton, the capital, despite rapid growth has managed to retain its distinctive charm as a clean scenic city of restful character, much like Cambridge in England, but like no other place in Canada. All principal streets are lined by sentry rows of magnificent elms, looking as if they were continually expecting a parade. Between them as you drive you glimpse lovely one-second vignettes of the St. John River.

It's no surprise, then, if so many former New Brunswickers come home with thoughts of periwinkles, dulse, maple cream, samphire greens and goose-tongue greens, fresh lobster and shrimp dancing in their heads, and if they go back to California with Christmas treats from home like barley toys, ribbon candy and English Christmas crackers.

And it's not surprising if former New Brunswickers, Dalton Camp, John Fisher and Charles Lynch, often hark back to their home province, as the late Ian Sclanders also did with such brilliance. Charlie Lynch, in fact, has written so appetizingly about the New Brunswick spring shad with fiddlehead greens, and Saint John Harbor salmon and green peas and new potatoes, and New Brunswick cheddar cheese, aged in foggy warehouses and possessing such a zing that it reaches all your taste buds, that Saint John people themselves have hurried to the old City Market to stock up while the supply lasts.

At the entrance to the market they always pause to buy mayflowers when the Micmac Indians are there. It's an interesting point: New Brunswick's provincial flower is the blue violet, but for some reason New Brunswickers are so fond of the mayflower that the Truro, Nova Scotia Indians don't take them to Halifax to vend, but to Saint John. The cry "The Indians are in town" brings out dollar bills among the New England Loyalist descendants, instead of muskets as in their great-great-grandfathers' day.

4 The Province of Peace

From his early boyhood in Argyleshire, Scotland, Duncan McColl was looked upon as someone destined to make an impression on the world. He was intensely religious and conscientious. Once he went surety for a friend on a loan, and the friend drowned. An acquaintance knowingly nudged young Duncan and pointed out he could importune he was not yet twenty, which would legally excuse him.

"No, it is my obligation now," he replied, "and I will honour it."

Over many months he paid off the debt. At twenty he enlisted in the British Army as a pay sergeant, and in 1778 was catapulted into the American Revolutionary War.

In the bitter fighting around Penobscot and Massachusetts Bay Sergeant McColl was wounded several times. When another sergeant marvelled at his repeated escapes in perilous missions, he said simply, "Divine Providence is looking after me."

The American rebels, according to local lore, had much the same idea about him. At Castine, Maine, where Paul Revere was in the assault force and Sir John Moore with the defenders, Yankee squirrel-shooters repeatedly nicked the scrambling message-bearer but even at short range couldn't drill a bullet through his heart. Finally an astonished rebel officer shouted: "Cease fire! God must have work for that man to do."

And the kilted youth dived and tumbled down a hillside to the safety of his lines.

That is the legend. Later, while stationed in Jamaica, Duncan McColl thought he had a vision. At prayer one evening the sins of his life passed before his eyes and a voice whispered, "Believe in the Lord Jesus Christ and ye shall be saved." This wrought a change; he found he could no longer hate his enemies, but instead loved all humanity.

Not surprisingly, he resigned from the forces in 1783 when peace came. He married Elizabeth Channal, a member of the Methodist societies of New York and Philadelphia. They moved to St. Andrews the next year, buying a log cabin for ten guineas, and then to St. Stephen, where Duncan McColl got employment as a clerk.

That first Sunday in St. Stephen he invited a half-dozen neighbours into his home for a religious meeting. The next Sunday sixty came. Word spread quickly through the primitive frontier country about the good man who prayed with people and how so many claimed they had "experienced the pardoning love of God."

From 1786 on, Duncan McColl gave much of his time to preaching the Gospel on both sides of the border. "Gave" is the word, because the Loyalist colonists were poor and he was not expecting to be paid. By horse and sleigh, by boat and sometimes on foot, he travelled endless miles. In seven years, he later recalled, his total proceeds consisted of a broadcloth suit of clothes he got for preaching several Sundays in Halifax, $3.50 pressed into his hand by a well-wisher in Pleasant River, Maine, and three cheeses which some Maine women gave him for his wife. He had to tote the cheeses on his back as he plodded ten miles along the beach of St. Andrews Bay, waded through several waist-high creeks, walked on to Robbinston, Maine, and then canoed to St. Stephen.

Parson McColl possessed persuasive and even inspiring powers. Some people credited him with performing a miracle on Christmas Eve, 1788. His wife lay critically ill in a coma and the doctor said she would be dead by midnight. Suddenly there flashed to Duncan McColl's mind the story of Christ going into Peter's house, rebuking the fever and healing the wife's mother. As he paced the floor, he thought: "Is He not here? Cannot He raise up my wife as well as her?" Something impelled him to go in and touch the bedclothes and look to her to regain consciousness. Immediately Mrs. McColl opened her eyes, and spoke; her recovery apparently began at that moment. Equally surprising afterward was her recollection that she had been dreaming, just before, about the story of Christ in Peter's house.

Ordained a few years later as a Methodist preacher, Duncan McColl might have served out his time unnoticed by history if it had not been for the numbing news that reached the border Saturday, June 27, 1812.

War had been declared between Great Britain and the United States. Not unexpectedly, next day's sabbath congregation was huge.

"The people crowded from both sides to our meeting house," Duncan McColl later wrote. "I could hardly make out to preach, with the people's sobbing and weeping, thinking withal this should be the last time they could see each other in peace."

The way the old folks tell the story that has been handed down from their grandparents, Parson McColl really took a pulpit-thumping initiative that day. He reminded his flock that for all those years since the last war he had baptized them, married them, buried them on both sides of the St. Croix River boundary. As all the families had lived together in friendship and harmony, he had no intention now of letting brothers and cousins start a blood bath, merely because the governments of two countries couldn't see eye to eye.

He told them the ebb and flow of the tides of war at this little border point could make no difference to the outcome of the overall struggle anyway, and he would seek a way to draw up a truce. Not a soul in the congregation objected.

On Monday, the preacher talked with a magistrate about the urgency of calling the householders of the district together. And a public gathering was duly convened and a committee chosen from both sides to oversee the maintenance of a truce.

It wasn't always easy to do.

One day he was preaching in Calais when a company of American troops came by. The captain and some soldiers entered the meeting-place and occupied seats.

Never had Parson McColl preached more earnestly. Explaining the traditional friendly relationship between St. Stephen and Calais, he entreated them not to do anything that might upset the peace. "It could be of no benefit to the cause on either side to ruin this country," he asserted.

61

To his delight, the company of troops went on their way without incident.

Then arrived Sir Thomas Samaurez, commander-in-chief on the British side, with some officers and men. Again the preacher pleaded vehemently for peace and goodwill and, almost to his surprise, Sir Thomas nodded agreement; he couldn't see either what good a massacre here would accomplish.

And the truce held, all through the bloody struggles elsewhere. People travelled freely back and forth across the St. Croix.

There were tense times. Parson McColl's constant goings and comings prompted cynical comment from some sources. Methodists were still regarded as dissenters, and many righteous citizens mistrusted them. Recurrent rumors circulated that the preacher was an enemy to king and country.

But then, suddenly, in 1815 the war was over.

No one in the border country had been killed, wounded or taken prisoner. No property had been taken by violence.

The story is told that an inspecting officer arriving from the British side was horrified to find the St. Stephen garrison completely out of gunpowder. He demanded to know where it had gone. The answer: "It was used up . . . the Americans in Calais didn't have any, so we lent them some to celebrate the Fourth of July."

So Parson Duncan McColl preached a thanksgiving service in Calais, amid heartfelt hallelujahs, and there were as many people from the Canadian side in the congregation as from the American side.

It had been a great victory for Parson McColl, and there was yet another great victory in store for him when on June 30, 1818, a new Methodist meeting-house was formally dedicated.

Many generations have passed. But if the dead could come back and look around today, no one would be more overjoyed than Reverend Duncan McColl – for the unique St. Stephen-Calais border point has become known over the world for the very kind of goodwill he preached.

Of course all along the New Brunswick-Maine boundary there are warm manifestations of international friendship. Madawaska, Maine, and Edmundston, New Brunswick, at times might be considered one city. Houlton,

Maine, often correlates special public events with Woodstock's Old Home Week. Perth and Andover, on the New Brunswick side, would not think of planning anything ambitious without bringing in Fort Fairfield on the Maine side.

But the example of St. Stephen and nearby Milltown, New Brunswick, and Calais and Milltown, Maine, on the other side, continues to be unique.

Water from St. Stephen is piped across the international bridge to Calais, relayed upstream to Milltown, Maine, and then back across the river to Milltown, New Brunswick.

Electricity formerly crossed the St. Croix River in the same way.

You can keep up your attendance record in Rotary by going to either the Monday meeting in St. Stephen or the Wednesday meeting in Calais – very convenient for "make-ups," local Rotarians say.

Any holiday on either side of the river is enough excuse to bring out the flags in both countries. On July 4 Canadians celebrate the American victory in the Revolutionary War no less enthusiastically than Americans celebrate the Queen's Birthday in May. Parades always cross back and forth on the international bridge.

When a fire alarm sounds on either side, the opposite numbers respond too and sometimes even get there first. A second alarm is automatically answered by all four departments.

Doctors from both countries practise on both sides of the river. Several physicians from Maine are on the board of the Charlotte County Hospital in St. Stephen. A Calais baby, born in the Canadian hospital, can still qualify as American-born for citizenship purposes.

In fact, there hasn't been even the semblance of a discordant note since the long-ago days when the driving rule on the Canadian side was "keep to the left" and motorists had to veer over in the middle of the international bridge or meet other cars head on. This was solved in the early 1920's when Canada switched to the right.

"If anything," says St. Stephen town clerk Frank Flagg, "the good relations and co-operation here on the border have grown even stronger with the passing years. The four towns are like one community of 12,000 people."

And so in driving through St. Stephen, when you notice the sign by a red-brick place of worship that says "Kirk-McColl United Church," spare a thought for the man who started it all.

5 The Amazing Comeback

"And it has all happened in such a very short time," Emery LeBlanc was saying. "Mainly in this century, in our own lifetime."

We were talking about the most dramatic development in modern New Brunswick history – a development so gradual, so unapparent to the eye, that some people did not yet realize its magnitude or its importance.

It was the emergence of the Acadian people from their long stay in the wilderness.

I had gone to Moncton one winter's day in the 1960's to see Emery LeBlanc, an outstanding student of Acadian history, former editor of the French-language daily *l'Evangeline*. It was fortunate I had his name and address before I picked up the phone on arriving, because it turned out there were 821 LeBlancs in the Moncton telephone book – a testimonial both to the fact that LeBlanc is the most populous Acadian surname and that Acadians comprise about a third of Moncton's 50,000 citizens.

And now, sitting in his livingroom, I found it hard to believe what he was telling me – that as recently as 1881 the Acadians in New Brunswick were hardly second-class citizens, let alone first-class. They were treated more as aboriginal peasants. They were poor, but not even on the poor-rolls like needy English-speaking people.

"Their only businessmen," Emery LeBlanc said, "were a few village storekeepers. They had one lawyer, a few doctors, and no dentists. There were only about five Acadian priests, the others were from Quebec and France, as in the early times."

A London travel book of the nineteenth century described the Acadians as simple folk who loved gaiety and amusement more than work. The author reported, "They form a race by themselves, mingling little. In the winter I have often seen them on their way to market with loads of frozen oysters packed in barrels, and moss cranberries; but they looked happy and comfortable, and went singing merrily to the ringing of their horse bells."

Emery LeBlanc added, looking out the window at the street, "In fact, the first Acadian dentist is still living."

"Are you *sure*?" – incredulous.

"Why, yes," he replied. "I saw him shovelling snow yesterday."

Subsequently I was to talk with the dentist, Dr. Antoine J. Cormier, a soft-spoken, pleasant man, about eighty years of age, who was one of several Dr. Cormiers now in the Moncton phone directory. Yes, he had been the pioneer, he acknowledged. He set up practice in Shediac in 1910 after studies at Baltimore and Philadelphia. A half-century later he retired, but his three sons meanwhile had all become dentists too.

In a sense this family personified the phenomenal twentieth-century transformation of the Acadians.

Today, with their burgeoning centres of higher learning injecting an annual stream of lawyers, engineers, doctors, dentists and other professional men into New Brunswick life, and with their businessmen increasing in number and influence, the Acadians are closing the gap double-quick between the way they exist and the way the "English" live.

How did their isolation begin? What caused the Acadians to become collective recluses for more than two centuries? Was it something imposed by the dominant English-speaking majority? Or was it a voluntary exile?

The answer lies back in the days when the first French settlers came to the land known as Acadia. The origin of the name itself is lost in antiquity; the early exploration maps of Gastaldi (1548) and Zaltieri (1566) showed it as Larcadia. Champlain, a half-century later, called it Arcadia, and a decade afterward changed it to Acadie.

If France had been a more determined colonizer, the history of North America might have been completely different. But in the early 1600's, when Charles de la Tour brought families from Normandy, these later to be supplemented by settlers from Poitou, Touraine and other provinces sponsored by la Tour's rival seigneur, d'Aulnay Charnisay, the influx was slow. Three-quarters of a century after it began, there were still only 915 people in Acadia. They lived mainly on a ribbon of land extending from Port Royal, the present Annapolis Royal in Nova Scotia, to Hillsborough, Memramcook and Moncton in New Brunswick.

Meanwhile England was pouring settlers into New England and southward. When Acadia passed the 60,000 population level, the English colonials numbered an overwhelming 1,200,000, or twenty times as many.

The ratio already foreshadowed the future. But the most significant event of that first century of colonization was not population growth.

"Acadia changed hands at least nine times," said Emery LeBlanc. "It was a pawn of the big powers. In 1613 Argall destroyed Port Royal. The French later regained possession, but soon the region was granted to Sir William Alexander, who tried to establish Scottish settlers. In 1632 the land was returned to France, but in 1654 the English became masters for a third time. Then in 1667 the Treaty of Breda returned Acadia to France, only to be taken over again in 1713 by the English under the terms of the Treaty of Utrecht. Only Louisbourg was given back to France. This fortress was captured by the New Englanders a generation later in 1745; it was returned to France by the Treaty of Aix-la-Chapelle in 1748, and captured again by the British in 1758.

"Can you realize the impact on the Acadians? They cared little for whatever government was in power, even less for the mother country. They had come to a new land which they had made their own, and they wanted to live and prosper. They wanted to be left alone. They wished the people in Europe would get together and settle their differences somewhere else. But they wished in vain.

"Acadia was a football with which France and England played. Imagine, if from the day of Confederation, Canada and the United States had fought over the Maritime Provinces and we had changed allegiance nine times: What mentality would we have? – a listless, passive attitude, a permanent inferiority complex, which when aggravated can easily become a persecution complex.

"Only one thing the Acadians always proclaimed: They could not take up arms against other French people. And there we have the seeds of what became the Expulsion of the Acadians."

That was only too true. The approach of the expulsion had been heralded for three-quarters of a century by the ferocious, bloody attacks on New England settlements by Acadian Indians led by French army officers. Sometimes more than one hundred men, women and children were cut down by hatchets. It was natural that the English blamed the placid Acadian folk, along with the French military. But the simple-living Acadians could never understand the viciousness of English fleets that sailed up from Boston to put the torch to buildings and slay their livestock in response to the relentless outcry in New England to burn out the wasps' nest in Acadia.

When many Acadians repeatedly refused to take the oath of allegiance to the English king lest they might have to fight Frenchmen some day, the colonial authorities feared for the safety of the British immigrants now arriving in their midst.

So in 1755 the great expulsion came. While about 6,000 Acadians fled up the coast or into the woods, another 6,000 were rounded up by the New England troops under command of Colonel Robert Monckton – whose name without the "k" is borne today, ironically, by not only the chief Acadian community but also by the steadily-developing University of Moncton which is the catalyst of Acadian dreams for the future.

Not everyone relished the job Governor Lawrence had given them. Colonel John Winslow, next to Monckton, told the Acadians of Grand Pré in his proclamation: "The duty I am now upon, though necessary, is very disagreeable to my make and temper." Brook Watson, the peg-leg soldier destined for great prominence later in London, called it in a letter "this painful affair" and said the rush caused by the advanced season may have resulted in families being sent to different parts of the world "notwithstanding all possible care was taken to prevent it." On the other hand many New England soldiers had neither sympathy nor even human consideration for the uprooted Acadians. One of Winslow's captains wrote: "You know our soldiers hate them, and if they can find a pretence to kill them they will."

Shiploads of Acadians were scattered all the way down the coast to Louisiana, and some were even shipped to France itself. Belle-Isle-En-Mer, seven miles off the coast of Brittany, is today the principal Acadian village in France, and very proud of its traditions.

But surely no race in history has shown a more tenacious will to come back than these Acadians. Three thousand of the expelled straggled home somehow over the next few months and years, on foot and by canoe, through uncharted forest, by small schooners dodging in and out of uninhabited coves up the Atlantic coast. Some trudged a long circuitous route to Quebec and finally down the St. John River. They were only to find that the harassed French commander, Sieur de Boishébert, who was attempting a last-ditch holding operation at the Evandale narrows, following the capture of Fort Beauséjour and the razing of the strongpoint at Saint John, was unable even to begin feeding and clothing such an invasion of hollow-eyed humanity.

Worse, they had stumbled headlong into yet another of the interminable wars between England and France – this time in such a barbarous climate that an unrestrained company of New England Rangers killed and scalped six French women and children at St. Anne's (Fredericton), and Governor Lawrence officially ordained a reward of £30 for an enemy Indian captured alive, £25 for the scalp of an Indian male over sixteen and £25 for a woman or child turned over to the English. Even though apologists tried to reason that le Loutre and other French authorities had put up rewards in the past for Indians who could produce English scalps, Lawrence's formal offer of scalp and body bounties ("to be Paid by the Commanding Officer at any of His Majesty's Forts in the Province") was bitterly criticized by more moderate New Englanders.

One band of Acadians came home startlingly fast. An English transport brig en route to South Carolina with thirty-two dispossessed families was, to the surprise of the captain, captured by the captives during an exercise period on deck. Experienced seaman Charles Belliveau guided the ship back to Saint John. Furious, Governor Lawrence despatched an English schooner from Halifax to recapture the brig and captives. Under the guise of French colours the ship sailed into the harbour of Saint John, the Rangers aboard dressed as French soldiers. Four French deserters took a small boat ashore to announce that the vessel had brought supplies from Louisbourg. However, the English accidentally disclosed their identity too soon and the schooner had to retreat empty-handed.

But the inexorable pressure of American Loyalist settlers, backed by guns, steadily drove the Acadians farther up the east and north coasts of New Brunswick and also up into the Madawaska County panhandle – squeezed between Quebec and Maine – the legendary "Republic of Madawaska."

Perhaps the greatest contrast between the Acadians and the Anglo-Saxons who displaced them was in their relative degrees of schooling. The Loyalists from New England composed an educational élite. They brought with them one-sixth of the living graduates of Harvard University and an equal number of alumni of other colleges, four hundred altogether. The Acadians were pitifully unlettered. There were no university graduates among them; it is questionable whether many of the young people could read at all. Even a century and a half later, in 1933 for instance, it is doubtful whether the Acadians could count four hundred college graduates among their entire population. It is in comparatively recent years that their remarkable educational upsurge has moved into high gear.

Between the Acadian Expulsion and the migration of the United Empire Loyalists to New Brunswick only twenty-eight years elapsed. By a strange turn of fate one of the Acadians whom England exiled came back to help hold Acadia for England in that struggle – the American Revolutionary War.

He was Reverend Joseph Mathurin Bourg, an extraordinarily influential priest among the Indians. Father Bourg – normally regarded as an Acadian but of Irish descent on his father's side – the name having originally been Bourque or Burke – was born in the Minas district, Nova Scotia, in 1744. As a child he fled with his family to escape deportation, found refuge in Prince Edward Island,

and was eventually moved by the British to northern France. He took up his studies in St. Malo, and subsequently returned to this continent as the first native Acadian missionary.

A few years after his homecoming a new kind of storm broke over North America: Americans versus British, English-speaking versus English-speaking – which greatly puzzled the Acadian Indians, to whom it seemed like a son fighting his father.

Both sides unashamedly played the game of wooing Indian allies by blandishments. There was nothing like war to bring out the spirit of brotherhood in the white man. Even as former French governors had sent glowing missives to the Acadian savages beginning "To our Brave Brothers, the Illustrious Sagamores . . . ." now the anxious English commanders addressed them, "Our Dear Brothers, the Principal Chieftains . . . ." and George Washington, on the historic eve of crossing the Delaware, took time out to pen a warmly solicitous message to the border Indians, "Brothers of Passamaquoddia . . . !"

Gifts for the Indians flowed as abundantly as the St. John River in freshet. Washington very nearly won them over; agents of the Revolutionary Congress in 1778 persuaded the Maliseets to supply six hundred warriors.

Immediately the tribesmen began attacking English vessels on the river, plundering farms, killing cattle. To Fort Howe on a rocky hilltop in Saint John they sent back the King's flag, with a ceremonial declaration of war dictated by rebel agent Colonel John Allan . . . "You know we are Americans and this is our native country. Americans are our friends, our Brothers and Countrymen . . . . What they do we do, what they say we say, for we are all one and the same family. . . . The king of England has no business, nor ever had any, on this River. . . ."

To meet the crisis, Superintendent of Indian Affairs Colonel Michael Francklin hurriedly sailed from Halifax with Father Bourg, the Indians' trusted Acadian friend and advisor, whom he had brought down from Bay Chaleur.

While they were heading for Saint John, a war canoe armada loaded with hundreds of Indians was moving down the St. John River toward the same destination.

At this tense moment the stark courage of one man stood out. A merchant, James White, who earned one dollar a day as deputy superintendent at Saint John, voyaged up the river to meet the oncoming horde.

Imagine the scene: ninety birchbark canoes filled with fired-up, war-painted braves – canoes so numerous they seemed to fill the Long Reach from shore to shore – and facing them, a single canoe containing a white man, alone and unarmed, holding his hand upraised to signify he was coming in peace.

The Indians respected personal bravery; they had also long respected James White as a fair-minded trader; so they gave him a hearing.

But afterward the chiefs of the Maliseets, Passama-quoddies and Penobscots couldn't agree on what to do. Head Chief, Pierre Tomah, asked for time to commune with the Great Spirit, and fell face down in the sand. For most of an hour, while he lay immobile, James White sweated.

Then Chief Tomah arose and broke the news: the Supreme Being wanted him to stay on good terms with King George. Some other chiefs demurred; they didn't think he had heard the message right; they wanted to attack Fort Howe.

While this parley was still going on, a messenger arrived from Michael Francklin inviting the chiefs to a great pow-wow at Fort Howe to settle all differences.

So for three days at the fort a talk-fest went on. Francklin and Major Studholme pledged the Indians the goodwill of King George III. Father Bourg produced a letter from the Bishop of Quebec forbidding any Indians to enter the church if they had harmed white settlers or defied the British government; he would "cast them out of the Church as disobedient and undutiful children."

Impressed now, the Indian sagamores turned over the American gifts and treaty to the English, took a renewed vow of allegiance, and sent to Washington a denunciatory letter dictated by their new friends. Then a gala jollifica-tion began with the distribution of English gifts to the value of $2,000, with singing, dancing, feasting and drink-ing toasts, and finally with cannon salutes and British cheers for the departing Indians and shrill whoops in reply. One result was the building of an "Indian House" above the Reversing Falls at Saint John, a truckhouse for trading with the Maliseets. All that remains of it is the name Indiantown, still applied to the neighbourhood.

Keeping peace with the tribes was something that Father Bourg, Francklin, Studholme and White had to work at constantly. The Acadian missionary lived for a time with the Maliseets at Aukpague, just above Fredericton on the St. John River, and played a leading part in a subsequent even bigger conclave attended by chiefs of many eastern Canadian tribes, including the Hurons and Ottawas.

For the occasion, and as a reminder to the Indians not to molest the King's mast-cutters, Colonel Francklin sent from Windsor, Nova Scotia, a varied shipment on the schooner *Menaquasha* to "My Brethern, the Chief Captains of the Maliseets – 250 pair Blankets, 40 Shirts, 4 pieces Blue Stroud, 6¾ yards Blue and Scarlet Cloth, 100 Rings, 200 Flints, 54 yards Ribbon, 5 cwt. Shot, 3 pieces White Jersey, 60 Milled Caps, 40 Worsted Caps, 50 Castor Hats, 100 yards Embost Serge, 100 Hoes, 1 Barrel Gunpowder, 1 Cask of Wine for the Squaws and such Men who do not drink Rum."

Among the Micmacs, too, in what is now northeastern New Brunswick, Father Bourg came timely to the rescue of the English.

The Micmacs' reaction to the tidings of the American Revolution was not surprising. They figured that the French would try to reconquer Acadia. And the best help the Indians could give them was clear to the Micmacs: they could massacre all the English settlers of the Miramichi River and Bay Chaleur.

When Father Bourg got wind of this, he summoned the chiefs and warned that if such a horrible deed were attempted, he would personally send to Hell every savage who killed a Christian; they would have ample opportunity to repent their murderous deceit while they were roasting. This effectively subdued the uprising – for the moment. Then the missionary noticed groups of Indians with their heads excitedly together. Scalping talk was apparently in the air again.

A squaw timorously approached Father Bourg and asked to speak with him. Luckily for the priest, he was a man who listened to all. She explained why the Micmacs were once more working themselves up to a ferment. In their uncomplicated way of reasoning they had struck on a happy idea for escaping the eternal fires. It was easy; kill Father Bourg first – then he could not send them to Hell.

Father Bourg fled to Halifax, not overland, where he might quickly be overtaken and tomahawked, but by canoe. The colonial authorities ordered out soldiers, saved the settlers, and rewarded the missionary with a stipend from the British Crown to serve the spiritual needs of the Indians.

For a century after the American Revolutionary War the Acadians, clinging to their language and customs, lived unto themselves in tightly-knit parishes where life centred around the church. If they lacked ambition, it was at least partly due to an ingrained apathy bred by long subservience, uncertainty, poverty, and suffering. New Brunswick Acadians claimed they could recognize an Acadian from anywhere else, including a Louisiana Cajun, by his lack of aggressiveness, his reluctance to speak up for himself.

By 1867 the Acadian population of the Maritime Provinces had tripled to 45,000 since the Expulsion. But they were not consulted about Confederation, nor did they expect to be.

The turning-point was 1881, the year of the first Acadian convention at Memramcook, which was inspired by a large French-speaking convention many Acadians had attended at Quebec the year before. After a day-long debate at Memramcook, the delegates decided to retain their own identity rather than join that of the French-Canadians of Quebec. They chose as their special holiday, not that of St. Jean Baptiste of Quebec, June 24, but the Feast of the Assumption, August 15. Later they decided on the blue, white and red flag of France, with a golden star in the blue, as the Acadian flag. And for the Acadian hymn they voted for "Ave Maris Stella," sung in Latin.

Thus they set their own distinctive course, seeing hopeful omens in that new Acadian leaders were at long last emerging and that the first Acadian college was now growing in stature.

What a vast change we find today! The original handful of Acadians multiplied to well over a million by the end of the first century after Confederation, 300,000 in the Maritimes alone, two-thirds of these living in the north, east and southeast of New Brunswick. There are even more in Quebec – about 350,000 – including several Acadian villages in the Gaspé peninsula. The village of Saint Jacques de l'Achigan, north of Montreal, is entirely settled by descendants of the returning expellees. New England has 75,000 Acadians, and Louisiana has 600,000.

From sixteen per cent of the New Brunswick population in 1871, they grew to twenty-four per cent in 1901, and thirty-three per cent in 1931. In every decade they gained another two or three percentage points until 1961, when the figure significantly rose by less than one per cent to 38.8.

What has happened is that increased affluence and urban style living have slowed down the birth rate. Acadian families, flocking to the cities and towns, want to be as comfortably off as their English neighbours. If the trend goes on, New Brunswick is unlikely to become Canada's second French-majority province in this century, or in the lifetime of anyone now living.

Some fretful English voices talk as if it will happen next month, if not next week. They claim the French are engulfing the province. They point to the noticeable spread of the French language in Saint John, where "never they heard a discouraging word" spoken on a city street before the Second World War. It is true that by 1970 Saint John's French numbered as many as 12,000 in a community of 100,000; but this was due to the Acadians' increased movement about the province rather than to any spectacular population explosion.

Perhaps the most remarkable thing of all is the recent social and economic headway made by the New Brunswick Acadians without explosive agitation. Quebec activists criticized them often over the years for being too docile, for not demanding and not issuing ultimatums.

But even if they didn't dynamite mail-boxes, which would have lost them the essential goodwill and co-operation of the New Brunswick "English," they kept the quiet pressure on, nevertheless – and it has got results.

New Brunswick became the first province to proclaim itself officially bilingual by legislative act. The two languages have equal status in the Legislature, in the courts, the public service, the schools. The Legislature was the first provincial House to introduce simultaneous translation facilities. The University of Moncton was established with "the unanimous consent of the English-speaking population and with their encouragement," as Dr. Alexandre Boudreau, director of the Memramcook Institute for Adult Education, happily recalls. Affiliated with it are the colleges at St. Joseph, Edmundston, Bathurst, and Church Point, Nova Scotia. There is now also a French-speaking Teachers' College in Moncton.

Because New Brunswick has advanced farther along the path to bilingualism than any other province, the present teaching institutions may be enlarged during the 70's to make room for students from elsewhere in Canada in federal pilot projects.

Has Quebec separatist sentiment established a beach-head among New Brunswick's Acadians? Says Dr. Boudreau: "We were expelled by the English in 1755 and abandoned by the French. There is an affinity culturally for France but it stops there – no sentiment involved. There is also an affinity culturally for Quebec, but the Acadians have been separated from Quebec for two hundred years, practically isolated, and they are not strongly attached sentimentally to Quebec. They want to feel at home in all Canada."

During Canada's anxious years leading up to Quebec's separatism-or-not showdown election of 1970, one of the positive voices speaking out for national unity belonged to New Brunswick's colourful Acadian Liberal Premier Louis J. Robichaud. Elected to the Legislature as a boyish-looking lawyer from Kent County at twenty-six in 1952, he set as his target to be premier by thirty-five–and made it at thirty-four on his first try. Thus he became Canada's youngest premier – but historically more important, the first Acadian ever elected to head a government in the United Empire Loyalist province. The Honourable Peter J. Veniot of Bathurst, also of French descent, had succeeded to the premiership in 1923, when illness compelled The Honourable Walter E. Foster to retire, but the Veniot government went down to defeat at the polls in 1925.

There is better communication these days between the French and English in New Brunswick, Acadian spokesmen say, and the problems and aspirations of the French are better understood than ever before. In Saint John, for instance, the predominantly English-speaking Arts Council sponsors an event-filled "French Weekend" of French drama, music, dance, lectures and bicultural social events every year.

One language both races understand is music, and the unique feats of Acadian university choirs, reflecting the people's traditional love of song, have certainly done no harm to harmony in the province.

St. Joseph's University (now the University of Moncton) and its ladies' college affiliate, Notre Dame d'Acadie, have more often than not brought home the Lincoln Trophy, emblematic of the top choir in Canada. Adjudicators have been enraptured by their "rich choral tone like a heavenly organ." One year in the national contest New Brunswick choirs, French and English, gained the first, second and third places. At the International Musical Eisteddfod in Llangollen, Wales, St. Joseph's won the folk-singing title in competition with twenty-four choirs from sixteen countries.

As is evident in their singing ability, ancestral influences remain strong among the Acadians. Because of their isolated history, especially in remote rural districts, they are more apt to retain purer seventeenth-century French words than Quebeckers – even if, by contrast, Acadians in bi-racial cities like Moncton may use more English words than Quebeckers.

In Lamèque, on the island of Shippegan, off the northeast tip of New Brunswick, you may find a farmer with little formal education who speaks a beautiful French, just as his forebears always did.

And occasionally you may discover a rustic Acadian home where for "seventy, eighty and ninety" they don't use *soixante-dix, quatre-vingts, quatre-vingt-dix* but instead the streamlined *septante, octante, nonante* as in Molière's plays.

But today's Acadians are not letting the dead hand of the past hold back their new-found progress. Look for example at what has become of the humble Assumption Society (La Société de L'Assomption), which in the old days regularly collected pittances from Acadians who had emigrated to work in the cotton and shoe mills of New England. Their spare small-change qualified them for $5 weekly sick benefits and a $100 death payment, and it included a nickel a month, later a dime, toward an education fund for their children.

Now the society has been converted into the Assumption Mutual Life Insurance Company, with head office in Moncton and a staff of four hundred operating on both sides of the border, with a growth rate three times the national average. It is possibly the most completely bilingual business enterprise in Canada – everyone speaks both languages – and today it sells to all religions, not just Roman Catholics. The company is becoming a major investor in the economy of the Atlantic Provinces. And not forgetting its original aim of helping Acadian youth lift itself up by its bootstraps, it provides several hundred university bursaries and loans.

General Manager, Gilbert Finn, an Acadian who is past president of the Atlantic Provinces Economic Council, points out that the company's swift headway proves that a group or a community doesn't have to have millionaires to get things done – "they can put up millions by getting together."

This then is the confident outlook of today's New Brunswick Acadians, planning their future in an environment of total equality.

New Brunswick is the province where the English-French population ratio most nearly reflects that of Canada as a whole. Perhaps it can give the rest of the nation a lesson in how the two founding races can live together.

6 They Blazed New Paths

A prophetic event was hailed by *The New Brunswick Courier* in Saint John on February 1, 1851.

Obviously the editor possessed the vision to realize it could be very important news – even if, in the fashion of the day, he published the story under the simple heading "NEW CARRIAGE":

A most ingenious description of carriage has just been invented and manufactured by Mr. T. Turnbull of this city, and during the week we are informed upwards of 1,000 persons have had the pleasure of witnessing it in operation.

The inventor has succeeded in discovering a motive power sufficiently strong to enable one man with ease to propel a carriage with himself in it at the rate of thirty miles or more per hour on a common turnpike road.

He has the most perfect control over the carriage. He can drive it backwards or stop it at once at its full speed. It runs on three wheels, the foremost one being the rudder or guiding one, the propelling power being communicated to the back wheels.

Mr. Turnbull has not divulged his invention yet till he secures a patent for it; but if it turns out equal to what is expected, we are of opinion that it will be one of the wonders of the age. We hope some measures will be taken by the proper authorities to examine it, and if found worthy, that means will be adopted for sending it to the Great Exhibition in London.

A horseless carriage clattering over Saint John's streets more than thirty years before the modern automobile industry got its start in Germany! Then why wasn't the wonder vehicle marketed? What was its method of propulsion – steam, gasoline or electric motor? And who was T. Turnbull anyway?

All the answers are obscured by the mists of time. An 1852 city directory lists a Thomas Turnbull as a carpenter. He could have been one of those fabulous original tinkerers who were not uncommon in the days when you needed only native genius and a good toolshop, instead of a multi-million-dollar technological laboratory, to invent something new.

Nor is it known whether he was related to another New Brunswicker, Canada's first aeronautical scientist, whose greatest feat was a milestone in world aviation history – Dr. Wallace Rupert Turnbull of Rothesay, inventor of the variable pitch propeller.

This advance – which Dr. Turnbull developed in Canada's first wind tunnel and on his own propeller-testing railroad before the First Great War – made modern air transportation possible. Previously, the rigidity of the propeller had prevented the operation of aircraft with maximum efficiency under different circumstances, such as taking off or flying level. He also did engine and propeller research that assisted the pioneer flying-machine experiments of his friend, Alexander Graham Bell, in the early 1900's.

Unassuming Dr. Turnbull, a kindly white-mustached old gentleman strolling about Rothesay on his cane until recent years, never did seek out the fame he deserved. But aircraft engine and propeller-manufacturing companies, which paid him royalties for years, are well aware of who transformed commercial aviation.

Another Saint John aeronautical inventor was furniture designer James Edward Fraser who, long before the world's first heavier-than-air craft took off, obtained patents for a proposed type of plane modelled on bird-wing flight. In 1908 he followed with a patent for a new type of plane with four vertical rotating wings. He was ahead of his time.

A gifted man of many parts – one of the most extraordinary personalities in our country's history – was Dr.

Abraham Gesner. A devotee of outdoor life, this doctor-turned-geologist came from Nova Scotia to New Brunswick in 1838, trudged and paddled all over the province for several years as provincial geologist. Before that job began to fade, he put his big collection of rocks, ores and fossils on display in Gesner's Museum in the Mechanics' Institute in Saint John – Canada's first museum. It contained also ancient books, mounted animals and birds; exotic curiosities brought by sea captains from all over the world.

His home was a curiosity in itself, for he had several Micmac Indians working as assistants, and every evening they would sit around a fireplace in the Gesner family attic, smoking *killikinick* and spinning tales and chuckling over jokes until they rolled up in their blankets and went to sleep.

Finding himself in financial straits, Gesner returned to Nova Scotia, resumed his medical practice, wrote a book about New Brunswick, delved into chemistry and discovered how to distill lamp oil from coal, calling it "kerosene." This burned with a brighter flame than smokey whale-oil lamps. It led him to patents, to fortune and to fame as "the father of the North American oil industry."

His private little museum in Saint John was the precursor of today's highly-rated New Brunswick Museum, with its vast collection of Canadiana amassed by another remarkable man, Dr. J. Clarence Webster of Shediac. Dr. Webster had a prominent medical career on both sides of the Atlantic, then retired to do historical research. The museum is notable for its numerous Wolfe portraits and mementos, lifelike Loyalist and Acadian rooms, and three-dimensional marine gallery, recalling in large windship models, paintings, figureheads and illuminated panoramas, the dramatic era when New Brunswick-built wooden vessels thronged the Seven Seas. Among the figureheads: a gaudily-coloured, reclining Marco Polo in Oriental garb – a relic from the wreck of "the fastest ship in the world."

Speaking of petroleum – New Brunswick very nearly won the honour of having North America's first oil well. In 1859 Dr. Tweedel of Pittsburgh cherished glowing hopes for his drilling project at Dover, Westmorland County, because oil seepage had been visible there since the beginning of time – primitive Indians used it for softening hides and mixing warpaint.

Then one day, after his ox-team-powered drill had bored down several hundred feet, a fateful letter arrived by stagecoach. Dr. Tweedell called his workers together and put the stunning news to them bluntly: "Colonel Drake has struck oil at Titusville, Pennsylvania. As we all know, one producing oil well is more than enough to supply North America's needs. So it's pointless for us to go on. I'm very sorry, gentlemen." (In later years the drilling was resumed there and a well brought into production.)

Not all New Brunswick inventors, by any means, managed to retire on their royalties. Among the luckless ones was Robert Foulis of Saint John, whose brainchild in 1853 was the first steam foghorn – an invention that saved countless thousands of lives around the world. His "coded" foghorn, initially installed on Partridge Island, made it possible for vessels to sail in new-found security. Even in dense weather mariners could identify the locale by the distinctive pattern of short or long horn-blows.

Like Gesner, Foulis was immensely versatile. He is said to have been artist, engineer, surgeon, engraver and foundryman. It is not clear whether someone stole his foghorn plans and elbowed him out of official credit, as he himself claimed, or in his many-sided life he just never got around to registering his accomplishment properly, because he was busy on newer things, like his own device for creating illuminating gas by decomposing coal.

But perhaps he was otherwise rewarded. Once his daughter Jean was travelling aboard a ship when a violent storm struck. Suddenly the mournful long-drawn-out *oooooohm-pawwwww* of a fog horn was wafted to their ears. Said a sea captain among the passengers: "The man who invented that fog whistle should get to heaven if anyone does."

Another inventor who died poor (of tuberculosis at thirty-five) was Benjamin Franklin Tibbits of Queens Country, a watchmaker's apprentice who was intrigued by the early river boats chuffing past his home near Grand Lake, and particularly by their simple engines.

After working in his uncle's machine shop in Montreal and reading every engineering book he could find, Tibbits arrived back in New Brunswick in 1842 full of enthusiasm for re-using the cylinder steam by constructing a compound steam engine. With some financial backing, he built the *Reindeer*, a paddlewheeler that easily outraced bigger and fancier river boats while burning less than half the amount of cordwood. He took out patents in Lower Canada, but was turned down in Washington because they told him the idea was not new, even though his engine design was original.

Tibbits installed his engines in several vessels, before being felled by illness at his home in Scotchtown on Grand Lake. Local lore has it that the evening he died, October 19, 1853, was the night the *Reindeer* burned, and that he watched the distant flames from his bed.

New Brunswick has had many other "firsts" – not all connected with technical developments.

Elsewhere in Canada it has been reported that coal-mining in this country began in 1666 with the finding of a considerable deposit at Quebec City. Actually the English ships that Charles de la Tour hired at Boston in 1643, as mercenaries to help break Charnisay's blockade of Saint John harbour, sailed up the St. John River afterward to load coal at Grand Lake for the return voyage.

The French built North America's first dry dock on La Coupe River, a Bay of Fundy tidal stream four miles from Fort Beauséjour – a logical thing to do, because of the stupendous rise and fall of the sea level. Nature would obligingly empty and fill the dry dock, if desired, as often as twice daily.

The S. S. *Experiment*, which tested her seaworthiness near Saint John in 1839, may have been North America's first iron steamship – a forerunner of those that finally doomed New Brunswick's wooden square-riggers.

The first newspaper of the New World was produced by the high-spirited younger members of the Champlain-de Monts expedition who spent an extremely arduous winter on Isle Ste. Croix between 1604 and 1605. These were the lively spirits who disdained "sitting around the fireside talking dolefully of Paris and its good cooks" and instead went hunting game by day and carried on intellectual pursuits by night – including establishing of a literary society which published the newspaper *Maître Guillaume* (Master William). The contents were news and light material.

The first penny newspaper in the Empire was established by George E. Fenety in 1838 – a tri-weekly, the *Saint John News.*

Canada's first English novel was written in Fredericton in the early 1800's by Julia Beckwith – *St. Ursula's Convent, or, The Nun of Canada* (165 copies printed).

Mount Allison University in Sackville precipitated a country-wide furore in 1875 by graduating Grace A. Lockhart as a Bachelor of Science – the first degree ever conferred on a woman in Canada. Many diehard critics expressed forebodings that the whole fabric of Canadian society and family life was in danger.

Canada's first rag-paper manufacturing plant was operated by Squire Wilson near St. Andrews.

The first paper made from wood was manufactured in Upper Sackville in 1839 – a portent of the day when pulp and paper-making would be the leading industry in New Brunswick.

One of the world's first Nature photographers was G. T. Taylor of Fredericton who, in the mid-1800's, even moved his darkroom into the deep forest. His large glass plates can be seen at the University of New Brunswick library. He also created a type of blueprint paper for photographic use.

Canada's first Baptist Church was built in 1763 at Sackville.

Canada's first Methodist Church was erected in 1790 at Point de Bute, seven miles from Sackville.

The first playground in North America was opened in Saint John by Miss Mabel Peters.

The first chapter of the Imperial Order Daughters of the Empire (IODE) was established by Mrs. John Black in Fredericton in 1900.

Canada's first YWCA was opened in Saint John in 1870.

Carleton County Vocational School was the first of its kind in Canada (1919).

The first consolidated school in British North America was opened at Kingston.

The first cable river ferry – winding in a steel wire on a motor-driven drum while unwinding it from another – was invented by Captain William Pitt of Kingston.

The first submarine cable in North America was laid

across Northumberland Strait between Cape Tormentine, New Brunswick and Carleton Head, Prince Edward Island, in 1852.

Commercial food-canning in Canada was started in 1839 by Tristram Halliday, who packed salmon in tins near Saint John.

British North America's first chartered bank was the Bank of New Brunswick, founded in 1820.

The first minister of public health in the Empire was Hon. Dr. W. F. Roberts in New Brunswick (1918).

Saint John also had the first fire insurance company in British North America (1801), the first biscuit factory (1801), the first industrial exhibition (1851), the first steam locomotive built in Canada (1858) – and, in 1826, three years before Sir Robert Peel organized the "bobbies" in London, the first paid police force in Canada.

7 A
Cavalcade
of Characters

Sarah Evelyn Edmondson, who grew up in the 1840's at Magaguadavic Settlement, York County, went away to the United States as did so many other New Brunswick young people. When she returned on a visit years later as a quiet-spoken, middle-aged, married woman, she told old friends she was enjoying life in her adopted country – which, of course, caused boys and girls in the house to yawn loudly because everybody knows that middle-aged married women everywhere live such exasperatingly humdrum lives.

One of the first things youthful Sarah Edmondson realized in New England was that men have a better chance in business than women. To get ahead faster in her job as a book salesman, she disguised herself as a boy. She got ahead.

She switched back again to skirts during the Civil War and, as a field nurse, joined the throng of interested civilian spectators who gathered ahead of time to watch the Battle of Bull Run.

This adventure-minded daughter of Irish pioneers, who had once wanted to be a foreign missionary, wrote graphically of the terrible fray that day:

Burnside's brigade was being mown down like grass by the rebel batteries; the men are not able to stand the terrible storm of shot and shell; they begin to waver and fall back. . . .
The tides of slaughter ebbed and flowed . . . then rebel reinforcements were mistaken for supports coming from

the rear of Griffin's and Rickett's batteries and the panic spread unbelievably fast . . . regiment after regiment broke and ran.

The grape and canister fill the air as they go screaming on their fearful errand. The sight of that field is perfectly appalling; men tossing their arms wildly calling for help; there they lie bleeding, torn and mangled. The ground is crimson . . . legs, arms, and bodies are crushed and broken as if smitten by thunderbolts. . . .

You'd think the sight of such a Union debacle would give any woman a stomachful of war. But incredibly, the next we hear of Sarah Edmondson she has volunteered for fighting service with a Michigan unit as Franklin Thompson.

For the following two years she soldiered as a man – again, incredibly, without being discovered. Many times she had close escapes from death. On a battlefield she chanced to meet a face she knew – John Vance of Saint John, a one-time admirer who had even visited her at home, but who now failed to recognize her. Private Thompson, overcome by remorse, decided to confess the whole story. But at that instant Vance spun around and fell, killed by a sniper.

She found that a talent for subterfuge became second nature to her – which wasn't surprising under the circumstances. She infiltrated the Southern lines on spy missions as a Negro, an Irish pedlar, a rebel cavalryman, and as a clerk.

To her astonishment, one day on the battlefield a dying soldier hoarsely confided in her ear: "No one must suspect I am not what I appear. Bury me with your own hands so no one will know. I am a woman."

Only two persons were aware of Franklin Thompson's real identity – an army chaplain and his wife. Eventually Sarah Edmondson entrusted her secret to another close friend, Surgeon Palmer, as she lay debilitated and sick in an army hospital tent. Next day he arranged for her to leave on a certificate of disability.

At Winchester, Virginia, while nursing, Sarah Edmondson met a Saint John lumberman, Linus Seelye. They were wed in Cleveland two years later, in 1867, and had three children.

It wasn't until two decades after the civil war that the

erstwhile fighting-woman applied for a pension. She wouldn't have, on her own accord. She was embarrassed at the very idea – but her husband insisted she was entitled to it.

Thus it was that in March, 1884, President Chester Allen Arthur signed a most unusual bill: "Be it enacted that the Secretary of the Interior is hereby authorized and directed to place on the pension roll the name of Sarah Emma Evelyn Seelye, alias Franklin Thompson, who was late a private in Company F, Second Regiment of Michigan Infantry Volunteers, at the rate of $12 a month."

Not unexpectably, this New Brunswick woman was the first of her sex to receive a pension from the United States Army.

Afterward she attended several veterans' reunions where her fellow veterans recalled, with new insight, that she had been nicknamed "the hairless boy." In 1898, at fifty-seven, she died and was buried in the Grand Army Section of the Washington Cemetery at Houston with full military honours.

Sarah Edmondson's story is told merely to illustrate again that New Brunswick has seen some remarkable personalities renowned for unbelievable exploits. They are a strangely assorted group – the most intrepid explorers and adventurers, the most outstanding traitors and rogues, the most courageous and ambitious, resourceful and far-sighted individuals you could find anywhere. If they have a common denominator, it is the fact that they are all uncommon. They rarely stayed in New Brunswick because most were impatient for the big chance. They helped build up every part of Canada and the United States.

The great Micmac Chief Membertou was one of the exceptions. He stayed – and stayed. It strains credulity to think that in 1534 he greeted Jacques Cartier on the east coast of New Brunswick, and in 1604 greeted Sieur de Monts at Port Royal.

He was an extraordinary Indian, this sagamore who was so wise, so tall, so physically strong and bearded like a paleface. Even in hoary old age the Chief was a splendid figure of a man and a fighter to instill dread in his enemies.

His normally calm temperament was inflamed when the body of Chief Pennoniac was brought back from Maine, where he had been killed by the Armouchiquois tribe while guiding de Monts and Champlain. Snowy hair tossing in the breeze, Membertou led the avenging flotillas of Micmacs as they paddled across high, rolling swells of the Bay of Fundy to the St. John River, to be joined there by Maliseet warriors.

Watching the great fleet – more than five hundred war-painted braves in all – set forth, each unit led by a district chief and Membertou in command over all, Acadian settlers admitted they shuddered, even though they knew there was no menace to them.

In a bloody battle at Saco the waves of invaders streamed ashore and Armouchiquois chief, Bessabez, and many of his deputies were struck down. Old Membertou led his birch-bark navy back to Acadia in triumph.

And speaking of giants of men, where could you find a more literal example than Paul Bunyan? Far beyond the well-informed bounds of eastern civilization, away out in International Falls, Minnesota, historians met a few years ago to try to trace the origin of Paul Bunyan legends. They finally decided he was only a myth. But up in northern New Brunswick it is well-known from stories passed down to succeeding generations that this massive man indeed lived, that his home was near the headwaters of the St. John River, that he was a French-speaking lumberjack who caused all his fellows to stop work and gape as he felled tall pine trees, one after another, with a few stupendous swings of his axe and that Irish and Scots lumberjacks twitted his exploits by re-telling them in magnified form. Very soon Paul Bunyan became a living legend.

How, then, did the stories spread West? They went with the New Brunswick lumberjacks who were seeking work and higher pay. The lumberjacks often crossed the continent to the Pacific coast, and back again. They took with them an expression, "the Main John," meaning the boss. It referred to John Glasier of Sunbury County, New Brunswick, who was one of New Brunswick's first senators after Confederation but also, more important to the lumberjacks, the undisputed boss of his vast timber operations and the first man to drive logs over the cataract of Grand Falls. You still hear the term "the Main John" used in some parts of the United States as well as Canada. And you still hear about that other well-known New Brunswicker, Paul Bunyan.

In all Canadian history there is not a more touching story than that of Madame la Tour, the determined and resolute heroine who commanded the defence of her husband's fort at Portland Point in Saint John harbour. The event was distinguished not only by her bravery but also because it represented a rarity in the New World's story – Frenchmen fighting Frenchmen.

Formerly a star of the Paris stage, Frances Marie Jacquelins accepted a marriage proposal by proxy from Charles St. Etienne de la Tour, thirty-five-year-old trading gentleman of Acadia. The reason was reportedly that she was now thirty-eight, if professing thirty-two, and other actresses were beginning to win parts from her. So in 1640 she sailed across the Atlantic into a life more dramatic than any role she had played.

They were married by a priest at Port Royal in what is now Nova Scotia. The witnesses included the other trading seigneur of Acadia, Sieur d'Aulnay Charnisay, and Madame Charnisay. Fate was to warp their lives into a peculiar pattern.

Unfortunately, Acadia is a long way from Paris and somehow the official commissions of the two men overlapped completely. Charnisay was to govern an area from Chignecto to Penobscot (which included la Tour's stronghold at Saint John), and la Tour was to govern the Nova Scotia peninsula (which included Charnisay's territory).

Then began a blow-and-counter-blow strife that went on for years. La Tour captured some of Charnisay's troops at Penobscot, then Charnisay seized the la Tours themselves and imprisoned them until a missionary pleaded for their release. Charnisay managed to discredit la Tour before the French court, and was given five vessels with five hundred soldiers to oust him. Meanwhile la Tour's friends in Rochelle despatched the ship *Clement* with 150 armed men and munitions and supplies, but it found the Bay of Fundy blockaded by Charnisay's vessels. Somehow the la Tours slipped through the blockade, boarded the *Clement* and sailed to Boston to beseech Governor Winthrop for help (incidentally throwing the thirteen-year-old village into a turmoil of fright at the sight of a French warship).

With adroit diplomacy la Tour was able to persuade the Puritans to let him hire four ships with crews and guns and ninety-two soldiers. It wasn't easy. There were great misgivings. Much prayerful talk ensued at a meeting called by the governor to contemplate the propriety of the step.

"It was argued that the speech of the prophet to Jehoshaphat in 2nd Chronicles, and the portion of Solomon's Proverbs contained in Chapter 26, 17th verse, not only discharged them from any obligations, but actually forbade them to assist la Tour," Winthrop's Journal solemnly states. "While on the other hand it was argued that it was as lawful for them to give him aid as it was for Joshua to aid the Gideonites against the rest of the Canaanites or for Jehosaphat to aid Jehoram against Moab, in which expedition Elisha was present and did not reprove the king of Judah."

Finally the improvised fleet sailed from Boston, and at its approach Charnisay's ships fled across the Bay of Fundy and beached themselves near his mill, which his men frantically started fortifying. But they were routed by a landing party of la Tour's men and New England volunteers.

Persevering, the chagrined Charnisay hurried to France to press his claims against la Tour, telling the king he was a traitor who had employed English soldiers in an assault on Port Royal. Charnisay returned to Acadia with a letter commanding la Tour to go to France immediately.

Not daring to leave the fort, la Tour sent his wife. Her mission was a failure. In fact, she was warned if she left France again she would be executed. Marie la Tour spirited herself to England, chartered a ship with supplies – and then had to endure the agony of a six-months voyage because the master, Captain Bayley, coldly ignoring her demands and entreaties, sailed up the St. Lawrence first, to trade goods with the savages.

When at long last the vessel entered the Bay of Fundy it ran smack into Charnisay's patrol ships on the lookout for Madame la Tour. Alarmed, fearing his vessel would be seized, the captain denied any knowledge of her whereabouts. As Madame la Tour and her attendants listened from their hiding place in the hold, Captain Bayley informed Charnisay this was only a peaceful ship heading directly for Boston. In a conciliatory gesture toward the New Englanders, Charnisay sent a message with him saying the French king understood that la Tour had misrepresented the facts to them the previous year and that His Majesty wanted to have only harmonious relations with the English.

The master breathed easier when the French sails slipped below the horizon. But he didn't take into account the formidable lady below decks, who was waxing more furious every moment to think she was again heading away from home.

Madame la Tour marched ashore at Boston, launched legal action against the captain for violation of his contract and, after a four-day trial, heard the jury award her two thousand pounds. Just as promptly, she paid out the money to charter three New England ships, loaded with provisions and munitions—and scorned the hazard of a blockade as she sailed back to Fort la Tour and an over-joyed welcome.

Like a fox interminably waiting for opportunity, Charnisay learned in February, 1645, that la Tour was back in Boston trying to get more aid from the colonists. Hurriedly he organized an attack on the fort.

The fifty men of the garrison, rallying around Madame la Tour's fierce will to resist, threw back the onslaught with well-aimed cannon fire, killing twenty of Charnisay's men, wounding thirteen more and raking his ship so badly it nearly sank.

Back he came two months later with a bigger assault, including two cannon he moved ashore to bombard the fort from the side. Madame la Tour and her followers fought back again with such effect that the siege force had to retreat out of range.

On the fourth day while the defenders were resting, a desperate shout suddenly went up: Charnisay's men were scaling the walls! A Swiss sentry had defected, giving the foe entry. Even then Madame la Tour mobilized a stub-born defence, but she knew her outnumbered band was doomed. To save those who survived, she submitted to surrender on Charnisay's pledge that all would be spared.

But she had forgotten how embittered, how hate-filled, he was. He had again suffered heavy casualties – twelve men killed, many wounded – and yet had been unable to defeat a woman in a fair fight. The only compassion Charnisay now showed was to offer life to whichever mem-ber of the garrison would hang his companions. Madame la Tour was forced to stand at the scaffold and watch the executions, one by one, with a rope around her neck.

Placed in confinement afterwards, she rapidly deteriorated in health. There are three versions of why she succumbed within three weeks. Madame la Tour's admirers say she died of a broken heart. Charnisay's supporters say the temperamental former actress died of spite and rage. Many people in Acadia and New England suspect she was poisoned by the man she had humiliated so often.

The tragic and true story has a surprise ending. La Tour, unable to return home, became a roaming exile. Five years later the victor, Charnisay, now holding unprecedented sway from the St. Lawrence to Virginia, fell out of a canoe into the Annapolis River and drowned. Contemporary historians say that when Indians rushed to the rescue of Charnisay and his servant, the one who grabbed Charnisay recognized him as the man who had soundly thrashed him with a cane only a few days before. So he held him under water long enough, on the way to shore, to make sure he would never do it again. The outcome was that the king soon appointed la Tour lieutenant-general of Acadia, and he reoccupied his old fort. When a problem arose with Charnisay's widow over property rights, la Tour solved it very simply: he married her.

Apparently, despite the fact that it was a union of convenience, as frankly stated in the marriage contract signed at Port Royal in 1653, they had a happy life.

And after all the terrible strife, all the hatred, all the suffering of so many years, four English warships bore into Saint John harbour the next year and compelled la Tour to haul down the French flag without a struggle.

But once again, in the end, the irrepressible Charles de la Tour triumphed. He sailed to England and placed before Oliver Cromwell his entitlement to consideration as a baronet of Nova Scotia. Many years previously his father, Claude la Tour, an ardent Huguenot, had renounced his allegiance to France and become an English subject. He and his son were both made baronets of Nova Scotia by Charles I, and they received a five hundred-square-mile grant of land in Acadia.

Cromwell honoured the claim. La Tour and two others, Thomas Temple and William Crowne, were granted virtually all of Acadia.

Weary of being a shuttlecock between two great powers, and rightly surmising war would soon break out again, la Tour sold his share to Temple and to his relief became a private citizen.

Yet even Madame la Tour's romantic story may not seem to some people as poignant as that of John Gyles . . . for John was not a grown-up but merely a child, and there is something inexpressibly sad about a little boy suddenly bereft of parents and cast into a cruel and lonely existence.

The lad was carried off as a slave by New Brunswick Indian warriors who, under French leadership, attacked the serene Maine town of Pemaquid. John Gyles, then only nine years old, saw his father, Judge Thomas Gyles, reeling before his eyes after being repeatedly shot. After the Indians led his father away with blood gushing out of his Sunday shoes, the boy heard the repeated *thwack* of the hatchets but, mercifully, the stoic man uttered not a sound.

This was John Gyles' introduction to the strenuous day-to-day life of the Maliseet tribe of the St. John River. Nevertheless, hard as it may be to credit under the circumstances, he came to understand and respect the Indians so much in the next six years that, when he was sold to a French family on the St. John River, he fled to the woods and flung himself to the earth weeping in utter despair.

His Puritan mother had warned him the French, who worshipped an alien religion, would destroy him not only in body but also in soul. Yet, once again, he ultimately grew so fond of the French household – who brought him up with affection and care as a son – that when the English came up the St. John River to burn and destroy, he hid his absent master's family on the far shores of Grand Lake and tacked a notice on the de Chauffours house that saved it from the torch – a notice that told how well-treated he and previous English captives had been here.

This youth, released in grateful appreciation by the de Chauffours – though they wished he would stay and let them adopt him – had become not only the first "permanent" English-speaking resident of New Brunswick but also, possibly, the first true Canadian in our modern context. He was perfectly fluent in English, French, and two Indian languages – Maliseet and Micmac – and could view problems, in their differing aspects, through the eyes of all of them.

But surely the most fantastic character who ever sauntered across the pages of New Brunswick history, duping everyone he met and laughing at locksmiths, was Henry More Smith. A confidence man, master puppeteer, hypnotist, seer, he was above all a superlative escape-artist. Chains, handcuffs, shackles – even iron collars made to measure by a blacksmith and stapled to the cell floor with chains – could not hold him. The sheer audacity of this innocent-looking English-born wanderer was his greatest asset. Few would believe that anyone could be such a barefaced deceiver.

He stole law books from Chief Justice Strange of Nova Scotia, returned them, and claimed the reward. From the Fredericton home of Attorney-General Thomas Wetmore, who was holding a dinner party, he made off with five top hats and numerous cloaks. Inns along his travel route complained that he forgot to pay for his lodging but always remembered to take the silverware.

Caught as a horse-thief in 1812 and imprisoned in the Kingston jail, he feigned fatal illness so convincingly that kindly housewives sent special foods to his bedside – one even sent him a feather bed to die on. While the jailer and a clergyman were heating a brick for his chill-wracked back, Smith vanished into the night.

More than once, when a posse was combing the countryside for him, searchers discovered too late from the fugitive's description that he had been a member of the posse the day before. (And had cheerfully expressed confidence the rascal couldn't be far away.)

It was during his second sojourn in Kingston jail, where Sheriff Walter Bates looked on him with admiring awe, that Henry More Smith demonstrated such an uncanny ability to break out of manacles. No one yet knows how he managed to twist the flat iron-bar collar from his neck – the bar an inch and a half wide – and draw the iron staple from the heavy timber floor. He tore the collar into two pieces as if it were nothing more than rotten leather.

Now, waiting for his trial for horse stealing – conviction would mean death – Smith pretended to be insane. He raved, roared, bent the rail around the prisoner's dock and then broke it. In his cell they found he had fashioned an elaborate marionette show out of bed straw and shreds of his clothing, coloured by blood and coal smears. Yet it was a delicately made ensemble of ten characters, who looked as perfect in dress and facial appearance and as gay of manner as actors on a stage, and who possessed jointed limbs like humans. As Smith, sitting beside the bed, whistled a tune, a puppet clanged a tambourine and all the characters gracefully danced with a symmetry and beauty which Sheriff Bates found too wondrous to describe.

Henry More Smith's genius so deeply impressed the authorities – and drew so many scientific-minded visitors from far and near, including the United States – that he received a pardon on condition he would leave New Brunswick. He obligingly left for Nova Scotia, and Sheriff Bates, to be certain, stood on the dock and watched the ship until it was a tiny dot.

One morning a few years ago, pupils attending the Kingston school noticed that a cot-bed in the teachers' room had obviously been slept in. The rumour spread like wildfire: "Henry More Smith is back!" The place was in a panic before it was learned that a teacher marking exams late had stayed at the school. Such is the enduring impression the great con-man and early-day Houdini left, even after more than a century and a half.

No one would have given you two pennies for the chances in life of young Brook Watson, a fourteen-year-old orphan lad from England who got a job on a ship sailing from Boston to the West Indies – at least not after a shark in Havana harbour snapped off the lower part of his right leg.

Back in Boston, the little cripple hobbling on a crutch joined a trading schooner going to Chignecto and became a clerk in the British garrison at Fort Lawrence. It was there that he was involved in a bizarre incident of the long "cold war" in the early 1750's between Fort Lawrence and the French Fort Beauséjour, less than two miles distant across the Missiguash River.

When the Fort Lawrence cattle forded the stream one April day to get to the greener grass on the French side, young Watson volunteered to go after them. Through their glasses, officers on the rival forts' ramparts watched him struggle across the frigid waters, wading and swimming – and then to everyone's dismay they saw his wooden leg sink deep in the mud every time he tried to take a step on the Fort Beauséjour side.

Suddenly the French officer in command muttered angrily: "That poor boy! My God, is nobody going to help him?" And a detail of French troops rushed out on the double to find a rowboat and help get Brook Watson and his cattle back across the stream.

Ironically, the boy with the peg leg was later given an important assignment, if a reluctant one, of rounding up Acadians for the Expulsion – reluctant because he hated to see the lives of people he regarded as simple, honest workers being disrupted so autocratically.

Brook Watson's star was rising as a London business-man when he was sent out to New York on a secret government mission before the Revolutionary War. Then, named Commissary-General of the British Army in America, he efficiently mobilized transport fleets to carry the Loyalists northward, became New Brunswick's first agent in London, eventually Lord Mayor of London, and a few years later Sir Brook Watson.

He had a macabre sense of humour about his wooden leg. In an inn, he would warn the servant pulling off his boots that "if you yank too hard the leg may come too." Having said that, he felt it was the servant's own fault if he was aghast to find that the leg did come too. Inevitably the servant asked how the leg had been lost, and Watson promised to tell him if he, in turn, would promise not to ask another question. The man hurriedly agreed. Where-upon Watson replied, "It was bitten off" – and watched the man helplessly puzzling.

Prominent too but in another sense were the two drink-ing companions of the Exchange Coffee House in old Loyalist Saint John, General Benedict Arnold and Colonel David Fanning.

Even though Fanning had been a ferocious fighter in the King's cause, few Loyalists could bear listening to his ceaseless bragging about how many rebels – often civilians – his guerilla force had slaughtered. It was as though the belligerent fighter was sorry the war was over, because all the fun had gone out of his life.

The story is told that Fanning, taking affront from a blacksmith's remarks, challenged the mighty man to a duel. For weapons the blacksmith chose broad-bitted axes; for the locale, the frozen surface of the St. John River.

Quite a large number of citizens assembled, in the confident expectation of seeing Fanning's head go skipping across the ice. But though the blacksmith was massive and powerful, he was also deliberate; and Fanning was lean and quick as a ferret. Faster than anyone had anticipated he leapt at the blacksmith – and sliced off his toes.

They finally got rid of Fanning – apparently by a means he might have thought ingenious had it been done to someone else. He was charged with raping a young coloured girl, found guilty and sentenced to death.

Strong suspicions prevailed that it was a frame-up. Fanning was expelled from the House of Assembly, where he had been sitting as a member for Kings, but Governor Carleton revoked his death sentence on the grounds that His Honour doubted the justice of the conviction. Cynics pointed out that Fanning had been a strong backer of the governor in the House, and said some other members, if convicted, would have got scant mercy. Whatever the rights or wrongs of the case, Fanning lived out his remaining days across the Bay of Fundy in Digby.

Benedict Arnold, of course, was a far more notorious figure. Nobody loves a turncoat, not even the side he turns to. And Arnold had the added liability of a testy, impatient and self-important personality. At the same time he was an able military strategist; the trouble was, he knew it. He served with equal brilliance on both sides in the Revolutionary War. After switching to the British and receiving his commission as a brigadier-general (plus $30,000 compensation for loss of property) he led the King's forces with telling effect in New England and Virginia, always under the shadow of speedy execution if the rebels ever captured him – which countless rebels were willing to risk their necks to do.

Why did he desert the American cause and try to hand over West Point to the British? It's questionable whether it was just money. More likely he resented that other officers received more official acclaim for their successes. And this may have been interwoven in a strange way with a feeling that it would be better for the United States to work out a negotiated peace with Britain, as the Continental Congress agreed in 1779 to do, rather than reach an ostensible independent status under the thumb of France. His apologists claim that if an agreement with Britain had been negotiated, Arnold might have emerged as a hero to the reconciled sides of what was really a civil war.

There is no doubt at least of the complete trust that George Washington placed in Arnold's generalship. "He is judicious and brave, and an officer in whom the militia repose great confidence," Washington wrote. Even after Arnold was twice courtmartialled for alleged misconduct and dishonesty, and Washington's intervention was needed each time to get him off, this trust apparently continued. Washington gave him the Philadelphia command and later, at Arnold's request, crucial West Point on the Hudson.

If Washington misjudged Arnold, Arnold also misjudged the British people and the kind of reception they would give him. He took his lovely young wife, the former socialite, Peggy Shippen of Philadelphia, to England, only to be snubbed by men he thought would welcome him. Even a theatre audience hissed him.

So they sailed to Saint John, where he fared little better. They had few friends, although Peggy Arnold was well liked. Arnold, now forty-four, seemed to have a knack of getting into financial altercations. In addition to his home on King Street he had a log pond in the upper harbour and a store in Lower Cove. When the store went up in flames the next year, a man who had formerly been in the business with him accused Arnold of starting the fire himself for the insurance. Arnold took action against him for slander – but instead of the $5,000 damages he sought, an unsympathetic jury awarded him twenty shillings, which was more humiliating than receiving nothing.

The more Arnold seethed and fumed, the more deeply he fell into public disfavour. One night a mob burned him in effigy outside his home. The blazing dummy bore a placard: "Traitor."

The Arnolds also tried living in Fredericton, a sojourn for which the general is remembered mostly for his deal with Nehemiah Beckwith, who built him a schooner, the *Lord Sheffield*, on the St. John River. Reportedly Arnold insisted on so many changes in design that Beckwith was a few days later than his contract delivery date – whereupon Arnold forced the builder to forfeit his penalty bond, leaving him in financial ruin.

Four years after arriving in New Brunswick, the Arnolds sailed away for the West Indies, later to go back to London. Here are some of the antiques, as publicly advertised, anyone could have picked who happened to be around that September 22:

Public Auction, at the house of General Arnold,
King Street, Thursday, 22nd September, at 11 o'clock,
if fair weather, if not, the first fine day:
A QUANTITY OF HOUSEHOLD FURNITURE
comprising excellent feather beds, mahogany four post bedsteads, with furniture; a set of elegant Cabriole chairs, covered with blue damask, sofas and curtains to match; Card, Tea and other Tables, looking glasses, a Secretary desk and bookcase, fire screens, girandoles, lustres, an easy and sedan chair, with a great variety of other furniture.

Likewise: An elegant set of Wedgwood Gilt Ware, two Tea table sets of Nankeen China, a variety of glassware, a Terrestrial Globe. Also a double Wheel Jack, and a great quantity of kitchen furniture. Also, a Lady's elegant Saddle and Bridle.

JOHN CHALONER,
Auctioneer.

St. John. Sept. 6, 1791.

It wasn't easy for anyone who felt rebuffs as keenly as Benedict Arnold – and yet invited them so much by his demeanour – to omit barbs from his letters. He wrote to Ward Chipman, New Brunswick's Solicitor-General, in Saint John:

London, August 16, 1792.
Dear Sir–

We feel ourselves much obliged to you and Mrs. Chipman for the kindly concern you expressed for the

100

sufferings on the voyage to England, and for your good wishes. We have the pleasure to assure you that we enjoy tolerable health, and find this country full as pleasant as St. John, though we much regret the loss of the little friendly society we had there.

I have taken the liberty to send you a small parcel, containing flannel hose, socks and a pair of gloves, which I beg you to accept. Should you again be attacked with the gout, you will find them serviceable; I most sincerely wish it may be the case. I certainly would not, had I the power to transfer the disease to some of my good friends at St. John. There is a small parcel in yours that I will thank you to send to Mr. Bliss.

Mrs. Arnold joins me in best wishes to you and Mrs. Chipman, and in sincere wishes for your health and happiness. Master George and Sophia unite in love to Master Chip. We beg to be remembered to Mr. Hazen's family.

> I am, with great regard,
> Dear Sir, yours,
> B. ARNOLD

But apparently the Arnolds were fated never to find complete peace and tranquillity. This is from a letter Mrs. Arnold wrote to a son of the general by his first wife:

I was greatly distressed by your father being concerned in a duel; but it has ended so safely and honourable to him, I am happy it has taken place. The Earl of Lauderdale cast some reflections upon his public character in the House of Lords, for which your father demanded an apology, which his Lordship refused to make. On Sunday morning, July the first, they went out a few miles from London, with their seconds, Lord Hawke your father's, and Charles Fox, Lord Lauderdale's. Lord Lauderdale received your father's fire, but refused to return it, saying he had no enmity to him. Your father declared he would not quit the field without an apology. His Lordship made a very satisfactory one. Your father has gained very great credit in this business, and I fancy it will deter others from taking liberties with him.

Shortly after the Loyalists landed, a twenty-year-old English corporal of the 54th Regiment was posted to Fort

Howe overlooking Saint John. William Cobbett was big for his age–more than six feet and weighing two hundred pounds–but what stood out most about him was that he was a teetotaller, he seemed to have little interest in the other sex, and he read scholarly tomes long after "lights out." He could recite entire chapters from memory. Nevertheless he was a mannish fellow, one who could march, paddle, and drive horses with the best of them and his fellow soldiers respected him.

Then one day, to everyone's surprise, William Cobbett discovered there were girls. He was sent with a communication to the home of a Sergeant Reid of the Royal Artillery and was dazzled by what he found – a young lady who was not only beautiful as he later wrote, but, "I saw in her marks of what I deemed that sobriety of conduct of which I have said so much, and which has been by far the greatest blessing in my life. I sat in the same room with her for about an hour, in the company of others, and I made up my mind that she was the girl for me."

William Cobbett, to put it mildly, was madly in love. The only small trouble was that this wondrous creature, this epitome of dutiful femininity, this Ann Reid, was only thirteen.

But nothing could dissuade him. One mid-winter morning he took a walk with two companions in the half-light after early breakfast, and there was the beautiful damsel, scrubbing out a washtub with snow. "That's the girl for me!" William Cobbett confided, as though it was news they hadn't heard.

After he got her oft-inebriated father's permission to see Ann, they would sometimes meet near the fort at a little fresh-water rock-spring where she went to fetch water, and they would talk about their dreams. (This spot, "Jenny's Spring," became so famous in later years as their trysting place that many have supposed "Jenny" was a nickname of Ann's. But the real Jenny was a woman who peddled water by the pail from this cold pure spring in the days when Saint John households were supplied by outdoor wells.)

One day William told Ann he was to be transferred soon to Fredericton, while her father's unit would be returning to England. He insisted she accept his life savings of 150 guineas – enough to keep her in an honest boarding house if her sodden father became unbearable.

Not until four years later did he see Ann again. Going home to England with his discharge, he was deeply touched when "I found my little girl the servant of all work at £5 per year in the house of a Captain Brisac, and without saying hardly a word about the matter she put into my hands the whole of the 150 guineas unbroken. Admiration of her conduct and self-gratulation on this indisputable proof of the soundness of my own judgment were added to the love of her beautiful person."

They married promptly, and William Cobbett determined they would become somebody. He studied French in France, then went to the United States to instruct French exiles in English. But he could never be an amenable conformist in any country. He opened a bookstore in Philadelphia and displayed portraits of the King and his generals in the Revolutionary War. The result – smashed window-panes.

Unabashed, Cobbett issued pamphlets maligning the reputations of Thomas Jefferson and Benjamin Franklin. He also charged that Dr. Benjamin Rush, who revelled in blood-letting, had bled hundreds of ill people to death, including George Washington. This cost him a £5,000 libel judgement. In fact, one libel suit after another was entered against him.

When an angry United States virtually expelled him, a disheartened Cobbett returned to England – to find that his forthright reputation had gone before and people were hailing him as a champion of free speech.

At home he proved to be as scorching a potato as ever to handle. He turned against Pitt and became his avowed enemy, espoused the cause of Queen Caroline against George IV, accused the Duke of York of hawking commissions in the army to keep his mistress in luxury, held up excerpts from Speeches from the Throne as flagrant examples of bad grammar.

When William Cobbett was repeatedly jailed, this martyrdom only raised his prestige higher in the eyes of the public. Hundreds attended a banquet for him on his release after two years in prison. And all the while Ann, besides looking after a large family, patiently waited for him and took food hampers regularly to his cell.

Once at election time, when he was standing successfully for the House of Commons, an innkeeper from

Yorkshire came to Preston to see whether the famed political storm-centre could possibly be the same young William Cobbett he had strolled with on early winter mornings in Saint John in Canada.

"When he found I was, he appeared surprised," wrote Cobbett. "But what his surprise was when I told him that those tall young men, whom he saw around me, were sons of that pretty little girl that he and I saw scrubbing out the washtub in New Brunswick at daybreak in the morning!"

As the years went by, accolades were showered on this rare commoner. Someone called him "the greatest of pamphleteers inasmuch as he could get a glad hearing whether he denounced Paine or Pitt, paper money or potatoes, whether he condemned the use of tea or commended small beer."

On his death, *The London Times* termed William Cobbett the most extraordinary Englishman of his age. *The Standard* called him the first political writer of the era. *The Morning Chronicle* eulogized him as the most powerful writer England ever produced.

The one-time boy corporal had penned an accolade of his own – one that meant much more to him personally. He wrote, as the years grew heavy on him, that all the happiness in his life had come from his wife Ann–the little girl from Fort Howe in Saint John.

Three youths went boating together on the Miramichi River before the turn of the century – Jim, Dick and Max – and anyone on the shore, watching these high-spirited country lads paddling along, couldn't possibly have imagined the impact they would make on history. They were all students-at-law in the office of Hon. L. J. Tweedie at Chatham.

Max Aitken of Newcastle was to become Lord Beaverbrook, world's most powerful press baron, maker and breaker of prime ministers, Empire Free Trade crusader, the human dynamo who, as Britain's minister of aircraft production, conjured up almost by legerdemain the planes that proved to be the immovable force to thwart Hitler's seemingly irresistible Luftwaffe hordes.

Dick Bennett from Hopewell Cape was to become Conservative Prime Minister Richard Bedford Bennett of

Canada, later Viscount Bennett living in retirement in England.

Jimmy Dunn from Bathurst was to become Sir James Dunn, internationally known London financier and Canadian industrial magnate, head of Algoma Steel.

And although Max Aitken had no idea of it then, he was fated to be a major influence in the career of another New Brunswick youth whose home was down the Northumberland Strait coast at Rexton, Kent County. Andrew Bonar Law – the only man from outside the United Kingdom to become prime minister of Britain (1922-23) – was, like Max Aitken, the son of a Presbyterian manse. But unlike impish Max, he grew up as a righteous, lonely, austere figure whose most exciting diversions were chess and bridge.

Law's political power helped Max Aitken win a seat in the House of Commons in 1910, only ten days after the ambitious Canadian youth stepped ashore in the Old Country. Max Aitken reciprocated by manoeuvering Law into the Conservative leadership in 1911. Subsequently Max Aitken masterminded the strategy that united the forces of Law and David Lloyd George and ousted Prime Minister Asquith, who was succeeded by Lloyd George.

It didn't take great foresight in the Newcastle of the 1890's to prophesy that young Max Aitken, the champion marble-swapper, would go far in business. When a St. Stephen soap company offered a bicycle as the prize for the boy sending back the most wrappers, innumerable young fellows asked neighbours to save theirs for them, and let it go at that. Not Max. One day his clergyman father, tall Rev. William Aitken, with the beautifully brushed white beard, was surprised to see a delivery van leave a case of soap on his front step. It was addressed to Max. The boy sold Surprise soap at wholesale to housewives everywhere – on condition they gave him the wrappers. In no time he was selling more soap than any store in Newcastle. Thus, without any help from home he soon owned a bike.

Even if his father couldn't see any sense in giving a boy money to spend on shows, Max was always right there in the front row when the Boston Comedy Company put on a performance at the Masonic Hall after a horn-tooting, drum-thumping, top-hatted parade through town. Max delivered handbills in exchange for a pass.

When it dawned on him there was something enticingly different about girls, arranging to meet them was no problem. He and his pal Hubert Sinclair signed up as members of the Band of Hope, an offshoot of the Women's Christian Temperance Union. This gave them the opportunity to sit in thrilling proximity to the fair sex and listen to lectures on the wickedness of the Devil's brew, interspersed with choral refrains in which they pledged life-long abstinence. Afterward Max and Hube Sinclair would repair to the well-stocked Sinclair cellar and the lifelong pledges proved short-lived.

You just couldn't get ahead of young Max. Oldtimers recall he kept hens as a profit-making hobby, and collected scraps from neighbours to feed them. Once, it is said, the demand for eggs far outran the supply – but Max supplied the eggs anyway. Some people were so unkind as to say he got them from his mother's ice-box. The story goes that a customer said to the boy the next day, "Are you sure those eggs were fresh?" And, after Max innocently replied in the affirmative, the man said, "Well, it's the first time I ever bought fresh eggs that were hardboiled."

It was in Newcastle that Max Aitken–eventually to become the publisher of *The London Daily Express*, which had the biggest circulation in the world – launched his original newspapers.

The first was printed in *The Advocate* plant when the schoolboy was only ten. Its most impressive feature was its motto: "We lead, let others follow who can." Only one issue came off the press. His subsequent venture, a little paper called *The Northumberland News*, printed at Millerton, folded too.

But the boy was unquenchable. He made money out of newspapers in spite of his failures by representing *The Saint John Sun* in the Newcastle area. First he got himself a job as principal newsboy. Then an extra job as subscription salesman. Not content with two roles, he became the *Sun's* local news correspondent as well.

All this before he was 15.

Later Max Aitken worked as a cub reporter in Saint John. No doubt there were times as he trod the cobblestoned streets, a short and unimpressive-looking youth in a well-worn suit, that he walked by a swaying and jolting junkwagon on which rode another smallish boy, even more humbly dressed, sitting beside his father. If the boy on the cart did not realize he was passing the future Lord Beaverbrook, neither did the boy on the street know he was passing the future Hollywood tycoon of tycoons, Louis B. Mayer.

By an odd coincidence, one of the MGM magnate's longest shining stars, Walter Pidgeon, grew up in Saint John only a few blocks from where the Mayer family lived. It was here in his native city, at the old Imperial Theatre, that Walter Pidgeon performed in public for the first time, singing "Blow, Blow, Thou Wintry Wind" during a First World War patriotic rally – unable to hear his own voice because his knees were knocking together so loudly.

Today the city is represented by yet another rising film luminary, Donald Sutherland.

Some of the headliners of New Brunswick history were notable for their triumphs, some for their glorious defeats. Among these was certainly Henry George Clopper Ketchum, a far-seeing civil engineer who knew he could solve the perpetual problem of the lack of a ship waterway across the Chignecto Isthmus which joins New Brunswick and Nova Scotia.

A Chignecto Canal had been a beckoning vision ever since the earliest Acadian days. It would telescope the marine freight-carrying distance between the Bay of Fundy and the St. Lawrence, and between the St. Lawrence and the Atlantic ports of the United States. Repeatedly promised, it almost became a reality – only to be frustrated by the devious twists and turns of political expediency.

Ketchum offered to build a ship railway across the isthmus that would serve the same purpose – for a third of the cost, or about $4,000,000. The idea made engineering sense, economic sense. What a crescendo of excitement swelled up around it! Ottawa politicians and London financiers were equally enthusiastic over the concept – a seventeen-mile line to transport vessels of up to 5,000 tons. In 1887 the great project was launched amidst oratory, handshakes and applause. Gigantic hydraulic lift equipment was brought from England. At one stage 4,000 men were at work. And then, like a house of cards, the whole thing collapsed, beginning with the financial misfortunes of the London bankers.

Ketchum one day was fatally seized by heart disease after a conference with his Amherst lawyer. He got one wish – he was buried at Tidnish, close by the proposed terminal. But later the high tides of the head of Fundy kept edging closer to the grave, and Henry George Clopper Ketchum, still the star-crossed loser, was moved by his widow's instructions to an unmenaced inland cemetery in Sackville.

A somewhat less magnificent failure was Charles Connell of Woodstock, who was too decent a man to try to sluff off on somebody else the blame for the New Brunswick five-cent stamp that bore his own bewhiskered image. The ridicule that greeted the appearance of the stamp in 1861 forced him to resign as postmaster-general.

There are three theories as to why Connell's face appeared on the stamp: 1. He ordered it himself to please an adoring young daughter; 2. the engraver suggested the idea as in line with U. S. precedent; 3. the engraver, having no specific instructions, got in touch with Connell's secretary, who naturally suggested his boss.

Whatever the reason, Connell resolutely endured a barrage of criticism from political opponents and, worse still, the vicious personal attacks that came from erstwhile neighbours and friends.

To his credit it must be said he not only faced it all but offered for office again, and won. Subsequently he became Surveyor-General of New Brunswick and still later a Member of Parliament.

But history is a stern, implacable and oft biased judge. Ever since, Connell has been known to the public as the man who wanted to show off his face, and fell on it.

He's hardly more admiringly regarded among stamp collectors, who writhe in anguish when they think of the fact that Mr. Connell, distraught over the criticism, tossed half a million Connell stamps into a bonfire outside his lovely Woodstock mansion.

Half a million little pieces of paper that today would be worth, at conservative estimate, $500 apiece on the stamp market. . . .

8 Up the Down Hillside

No other part of the globe to my knowledge can claim to have both an upside-down hill and a waterfall that goes both ways. It is probably just as well, the state of the world being already what it is.

But these are just two of New Brunswick's incredible natural phenomena.

The waterfall, of course, is Saint John's renowned Reversing Falls, the boiling, frothing rapids that race seaward between sheer limestone cliffs when the tide is going out – dropping eleven feet to sea level – and, when the high-rise tide is coming in from the Bay of Fundy, reverse their direction, overpowering the river, and tumbling and foaming upstream just as rapidly.

Not only is the spectacle heightened by the force of the water being compressed into the narrow gorge, but the turbulence of the flow in both directions is intensified by the fact that the water is rushing over rock ledges on the river bottom.

It's a massive, frightening performance taking place twice a day. In Maliseet Indian lore this was where the god-hero Glooscap explosively smote the mischievous Big Beaver's dam with his club. A fragment of the club lodged in the falls as Split Rock, and part of the dam got snagged in the harbour entrance as Partridge Island.

Here the Indians sped gift-bearing arrows into logs gyrating ceaselessly in whirlpools of the falls, in the hope that the tobacco and beaver skins would mollify the angry Manitou, or devil, that was responsible for the fearsome sight.

Here too, in bygone days, fishermen on the old bridge above the Falls took advantage of Manitou's generosity and busily cranked hand-winches to reel up sea bass as big as sixty pounds.

And here in March, 1858, a stagecoach coming from Fredericton to Saint John on a gale-battered evening halted abruptly on the old bridge over the Reversing Falls. In vain did the driver lash his horses. Clambering down, he found the planking had been torn away by the winds. To go on would have meant almost certain death.

But an even greater vertical water drop by far is seen at Grand Falls in northern New Brunswick. This is the third largest waterfall in eastern North America. It was here that the remarkable timber pioneer, "Main John" Glasier, made history by being the first to send logs shooting over the falls.

And here was the origin of one of the most poignant tales of New Brunswick folklore – the story of how the young Maliseet mother, Malabeam, forced to act as a guide for the ferocious invading Mohawk hordes after they had killed her husband and children, lulled them to sleep and let their rafted birchbark canoes drift over the brink of this seventy-four-foot-deep precipice which the Indians called Checanekepeag, the Destroying Giant. Thus she saved the Maliseets' Fort Meductic near Woodstock, but lost either her life or her sanity, depending on which version you hear. Either she was swept over the falls to her death in the rocky gorge below, or she slipped away from her canoe in time to swim frantically to shore, her escape unnoticed amid the awakening Mohawks' puzzlement over the gathering roar downstream.

Whimisical Nature endowed the Moncton region in south-eastern New Brunswick with an enviable bonanza of oddities. On the seashore at Hopewell Cape, strange reddish rock formations rise like giant Polynesian heads eighty feet in the air – monuments sculpted by tides and winds and frost over countless centuries to fill the aboriginal Indians with awe and inspire their legends. The high domes of some statues are thatched with balsam fir and dwarf black spruce, which always prompts children to ask how the trees got up there.

At Demoiselle Creek a few miles from Hillsborough is a subterranean lake of undetermined size, low-roofed by dripping stone icicles. The white gypsum floor of the lake emerges startlingly visible through the clear water. To step into the cavern entrance on a hot summer day is like unexpectedly walking into a cold-storage plant.

When you first glimpse the Petitcodiac River at Moncton you may wonder why it is called a river as there is only a little trickling brook to be seen while the billowy, chocolate-blancmange banks are bare of water.

And then, suddenly, the missing water comes into view – a veritable tidal wave as high as five feet, fanning up the empty river-bed at eight miles an hour, like surf cresting up an endless beach. What causes this? The rapidly swelling Fundy tide is dammed temporarily by shoals at the river's mouth. When at last it overcomes these obstacles, the triumphant tide drives inland with inexorable momentum, sweeping everything before it.

More than one oil prospector, intently examining the shale in the exposed river bed, has been trapped by the incoming tidal bore, picked up bodily, tossed head over feet a few times and then flung up on the muddy embankment like a rejected morsel.

But if I had to pick a favourite natural phenomenon it would be the Magnetic Hill. This is perhaps understandable under the circumstances, which date back to a June day in 1933 . . . and how three young newspapermen recognized a story but failed to recognize a fortune.

Often the night staff of *The Telegraph-Journal* in Saint John had heard pressroom superintendent, Alex Ellison, tell a curious anecdote. It was about a clergyman early in this century who was bringing children home from a picnic. He stopped his touring car at the foot of a hill during a rainstorm to put up the side flaps.

To the good man's amazement, his car started to coast up the hill by itself – "the most astonishing thing I ever experienced," the cleric related. He had to sprint after it and jump in.

The unbelievable episode seemed so well vouched for that three of us decided one night to try to locate the hill. We knew, of course, this was a fool's errand. Only a fool would think otherwise.

It was an ambitious project in those days even to think of driving one hundred miles to Moncton over rutty dirt roads in a tiny open 1931 Ford roadster (which John

Bruce had paid $605 for, brand new – including New Brunswick license plates and financing charges). Leaving after the newspaper had been put to bed at 3 A.M., we found it was nearly six when we neared Moncton.

John Bruce, a former engineer, had brought his surveying instruments just in case. Jack Brayley, now Atlantic chief of *The Canadian Press*, at Halifax was ready to write the story – if we found one. I was carrying the office camera, an 1891-style Graflex the size of a soup carton.

Now began the frustrating process of trying one hill after another, on every country road within a radius of ten miles of Moncton.

We attracted quite a lot of attention. Every time John Bruce halted the car at the base of a grade and put it into neutral, nothing happened. But we could see lace curtains being pulled back in farmhouse windows, and occasionally we'd glimpse a nose or a pair of raised eyebrows. It must have looked like the end of quite a party, or the start of one.

Once a passing farmer herding some cows called out: "Need any help?"

"No," was the reply. "We're just waiting to see if the car will coast up the hill!"

The farmer kept looking back over his shoulder all the way to the next field.

Three weary modern explorers were ready to give up around 11 A.M. We were down to our last hill – a former Indian trail that became a wagon road, on a two hundred-yard gradual rise leading up towards Lutes Mountain.

Then it happened.

The car, in neutral, began coasting *uphill* – slowly at first, then faster. Elated, we all jumped out and almost let the roadster get away on us.

Any thought of magnetism immediately evaporated when John Bruce noticed the water in the ditch was running "uphill" too.

It was not difficult, from this premise, to realize that the whole downsloping countryside was tilted – that the seeming phenomenon was due simply to the fact that what appeared to be an upgrade for two hundred yards was really a downgrade.

Starting homeward, we turned into an intersecting road above the "hill" and came to a driveway entrance

112

where a little girl was selling home-made ice cream, five cents a dish, on a plank across two wooden sawhorses.

"Let's stop," someone suggested. "We're parched, and besides, she thinks she's such a smart little business-woman."

She was. If there was any keen business mind there-abouts that day, it belonged to little Muriel Lutes of Lutes Mountain. She was curious about why we had stopped the roadster at the bottom of the hill; she said she had never heard anyone mention that it was extraordinary in any way.

We went home, published our news feature and photos, and forgot about the phenomenon. But Muriel Lutes didn't. She grew up, moved her father's gas pump down the hill, married a Polish New Canadian after the Second World War, built up a large tourist gift centre and restaurant complex that now includes a post office by name of Magnetic Hill and a motel and a zoo and a riding club. It's the biggest thing of its kind east of Montreal, certainly the only one that keeps four dance bands busy in the summer. Muriel's business thrives on the motorists from all over North America who line up all day long – on a summer Sunday, more than thirty-five hundred – to experience the peculiar sensation of freewheeling up a hill with clutch disengaged.

Mrs. Ludwig Sikorski, the former Muriel Lutes, still spotlights her own home-made ice cream. And she still sells gas – at a place where cars appear to glide up hill without using gasoline.

Magnetic Hill has become a New Brunswick institution.

If the Sikorskis have one baffling problem, it's how to convince people when they tell them frankly that Magnetic Hill is an optical illusion. Most visitors would much rather find a way to justify the magnetism theme.

One Torontonian comes back every year and claims the electric currents help his arthritis.

A Californian insists he can sense the magnetism in his bones and has to use conscious force to focus his eyes. He knowingly asks: "Where do you keep the magnets?"

Another American contends he can feel the nails being drawn out of his shoes – so Magnetic Hill is unquestionably sitting atop great unexploited iron ore deposits.

Still another declares that as he walks up the hill he

can feel his eyeballs being pulled. If he does, somebody walking right behind him must be pulling them, because there is no magnetism in the hill.

Yet another tourist informs Mrs. Sikorski: "If it was only an optical illusion, my car wouldn't actually do it!"

How can you answer completely devastating logic like that?

9 Tall Timber, Tall Ships, Tall Men, Tall Tales

Flames shot skyward from beacon fires atop hills all the way from Richibucto to Chatham. Cannon boomed salutes. Church bells pealed a gladsome clangour. Children and their parents hurried from their homes to the roadside, the youngsters gripping flags in their tiny hands, ready to wave and cheer. Horsemen cantered from Chatham town down the dirt highway in the direction of Richibucto forty miles away. Something big was happening.

Was it the end of a war? Was it an imminent Royal visit?

It was neither. Joseph Cunard was coming back to the Miramichi from a trip to England. This was the gala homecoming he always expected and loved. In fact, he often stayed overnight in Richibucto and sent word ahead, so there would be no slip-up in arranging the enthusiastic demonstration.

For Joe Cunard was the master-key to the economy of the Miramichi and the North Shore and the east coast. He was the king of a huge domain and he personified the role to the hilt. No one in New Brunswick ever wielded more regional power, nor lived more opulently and ostentatiously. In Chatham he and his family occupied an expansive home amid a beautifully manicured landscape, where the peacocks strutted proudly among the shade trees. They drove to church like a state procession in a coach-and-four, attended by liveried footmen and coachmen.

What caused Joe Cunard to crave such adulation? Possibly it was because he was not the main Cunard, and he knew it and resented it. The leader of the Loyalist

115

family, originally of German extraction, was Samuel Cunard in Halifax, a man destined for enduring fame on the world's oceans. In 1820 he sent his brothers Joseph, Henry and John to the Miramichi to found a branch of the shipbuilding firm.

Joseph, then only twenty-two, took over the leadership of the New Brunswick enterprise. Almost before the countryside knew what was happening, the Cunards had launched shipyards in Chatham, Richibucto, Kouchibouguac, and Bathurst, plus lumber mills, brickyards, fish warehouses and stores seemingly everywhere.

In a region that raised burly men as a matter of course, there was no figure more imposing than six-foot, two hundred pound Joe Cunard, astride a huge, beautifully groomed horse, touring his gangs of workmen.

Though he could be kind, considerate and even generous when it suited him, Joe Cunard was also an utterly remorseless driver of hard bargains, one who exulted in the heady glee of trampling competition underfoot. He muscled the Shireff family out of Middle Island, which he wanted for an export fish-packing depot; A.D. Shireff fumed with hate all the rest of his days. On his deathbed, Shireff told Henry Wyse who came to comfort him: "I have my two pistols under the pillow. They're for Cunard – I'll get him yet!"

Appalled at such murderous talk from a dying man, Henry Wyse demanded he hand over the pistols, "and prepare yourself for Heaven." Shireff's pistols were to remain in seclusion, unloaded and unused, in Wyse's home until a fateful day far in the future.

But many a good citizen kept a weapon handy in those lusty, brawling days on the Miramichi, because it was more like a Western frontier community than the circumspect East. More than vanity prompted Joe Cunard, when he went clip-clopping on horseback through the forested countryside, to make sure his husky outriders "Galloping" Fraser and John Germaine were always with him.

Nor was it mere ceremonial panoply when a band of riders escorted his stage coach into Chatham on his return from abroad, bobbing up and down on their horses like a company of Household Guards accompanying the Royal coach in a Coronation parade, for you never knew when there might be a sudden violent incursion from north of the Miramichi where Cunard's business rivals, Gilmour, Rankin & Company of Douglastown, held sway.

The rivalry exploded in the provincial election of 1843—the "fighting election" as it is still known. A Chatham member of the provincial House had been unseated by Alexander Rankin. In the subsequent contest, Rankin recruited five hundred men to intimidate Cunard cohorts and prevent them from voting. Cunard characteristically recruited one thousand to do the same job on Rankin's followers. As the election proceeded more bricks and stones were cast than ballots as voters dodged in and out of the polls.

Then came the climactic "Day of the Siege." Like wildfire the word spread in Chatham that Rankin's legions were coming to demolish the town. Women and children were hurried to the country. Cunard's men braced themselves behind heavy timber barricades armed with spike-loaded cannon. Nine boats full of Rankin's men headed downstream from Douglastown, seemed about to land at the Chatham wharf and then kept going. No one ever found out whether they were frightened off or the whole thing was a gigantic hoax. Just the same, public travel back and forth across the anxious river was negligible for more than a year after Rankin's candidate won that election.

Joe Cunard reached the zenith of his prestige when he came back from England after his brother, later Sir Samuel Cunard, had succeeded in negotiating contracts with the British government to carry the trans-Atlantic mail on two steamships he promised to build.

The Miramichi greeted Joe Cunard as ecstatically as if he had done it himself, and as if iron steamships were to be the salvation of the New Brunswick wooden ship-building industry instead of its nemesis. Carpenters, shipwrights, hammermen, jointers, riggers, trade after trade, group after group joined the banner-waving parade that made a formal presentation next day to a not-unwilling Joseph Cunard, and expressed heartfelt gratitude for all he was doing for the Miramichi.

For a time Joseph Cunard lived in Richibucto, which had become New Brunswick's third leading shipbuilding centre. His two sons, one subsequently well known in British politics, went to school there. So did David Jardine, who, years afterward, became chairman of the board of the Cunard Steam-ship Company. And a later scholar was Bonar Law, who made history as the first man from outside the United Kingdom to become Prime Minister of Britain.

To the common people, the Cunard dynasty was an aristocracy on the demi-god level. It had five hundred men building ships at Chatham and elsewhere, and it launched one ship somewhere every fortnight. Its operations were expanding all the time. Everything it touched turned to gold.

But, abruptly and stunningly, the golden touch was lost. A letter that came from England in 1848 caused Joseph Cunard to go chalk-white, and he hastened on horseback to his estate. In a trice, everybody knew. Joseph Cunard had failed. He couldn't borrow any more to keep his ubiquitous enterprises going, and to keep selling more timber than Alexander Rankin.

Human nature being the mercurial thing it is, the town's streets filled with alarmed people shaking their fists and demanding to know from Joseph Cunard about their jobs. Some shouted "Shoot him!"

Amidst them, slowly, with dignity and aplomb, rode the erect old man, oblivious of the threats. He espied little William Wyse in the throng. "Go to your father," he ordered, "and tell him to bring the loaded pistols down."

The boy scampered away while Cunard, sitting erect, his expression immobile, faced the rumbling menacing crowd. Then Willie Wyse came stumbling back, breathless, and handed him the pistols.

Deliberately, old Joe Cunard gripped one in each hand – the pistols that were once meant to slay him. In a clear ringing voice he called out: "Now show me the man who would shoot Cunard!"

A long silence . . . and then, slowly the crowd began to disperse. In defeat, Joe Cunard had won.

He rode away that night forever, to die seventeen years later in Liverpool, England. His debts were paid over the period of the next quarter-century by the Cunard family. As a homespun Miramichi balladeer memorialized it:

At dark on the Richibucto Road
No cannons boomed, or beacons glowed.
A man rode alone through the gathering night,

With the frogs for band, and the stars for light.
Wrapped in his cloak, with his head bent down,
Joe Cunard is leaving town.

The great timberlands, which still cover eighty-five per
cent of New Brunswick, have always been the economic
bulwark of the province. There wouldn't have been a shipbuilding boom in the last century without abundant
versatile wood. But what a revolutionary sequence of
changes the forest industry has gone through!

Originally, the only potential anyone saw was in the
pine – the seemingly limitless stands of straight white pine
reaching skyward. The French were shipping pine for navy
masts as early as 1700, when the man-of-war *Avenant* took
a cargo from Saint John.

Three-quarters of a century later the new proprietors of
Acadia, the English, sent Nova Scotia Surveyor-General
Charles Morris on a field trip to seek pine sticks for the
Royal Navy. He found few in what is now Nova Scotia,
but tremendous quantities on the St. John River and its
tributaries. In what must have been the understatement of
the year, Morris referred also to "a black spruce, fit for
yards and topmasts, and other timber fit for shipbuilding."

Tall pine was valuable. A seventy-foot mast, eighteen
inches in diameter, was worth £10 but a 108-foot mast,
thirty-six inches in diameter, fetched £136. Especially
designed "mast ships" carried the big timbers to England.
They were also highly popular among passengers, as they
were always well convoyed.

Massive pines grew near Blagdon Station. Philip Nase
floated one down the St. John River and sold it to a Captain Buttress, who debated a perplexing question with
himself. Should he cut off part of the big stick to get it
safely aboard, or make a hole in the master's cabin? He
decided to remodel his quarters and, being a philosophical
man, used the butt end in his cabin as a table.

Tempers flared in New Brunswick, especially after the
Loyalists came, when the King's agents insisted on marking with "the broad arrow" any pine of twenty-four inches
or more diameter found on granted land. This mark reserved the tree for the Royal Navy.

It is easy to understand Whitehall's concern about
keeping the navy strong. At the same time the new settlers

of New Brunswick, loyal as they were, didn't want to be harassed beyond reason. Their sentiments had been aptly voiced years before by Colonel Alexander McNutt on a visit to London:

It makes but little difference to the farmer what kind of timber or wood be reserved, whether white pine, gopher or shittim wood (if there be any reservation at all) as his lands will always be reliable to forfeiture at the pleasure of the informer, who may be a knight of the post ready to swear to anything and everything to answer his purpose . . . . It cannot be expected that any farmer will let any tree grow to that size . . . . Consequently he will destroy all the young growths.

But not until 1811 did the settlers win out: the law was rescinded.

Long ere this, everyone had begun to realize that pine wasn't everything. Ships were being built in New Brunswick at an accelerating rate because Britain, faced by increasing hostility from Russia, Denmark and Sweden, had not been able to depend on timber from the Baltic. In fact, Scott Brothers of Greenock, after rejecting alternatives of bringing timber from the Mediterranean, or setting up a plant near the last stands of English oak, hit on the idea in 1799 of sending out a complete shipbuilding unit of artisans to start a branch in Saint John. It was headed by the youngest Scott Brother, Christopher. They brought their own copper spikes, rigging, hawsers and other needs – even numerous, high-quality linen shirts which were to be given to helpful colonial officials.

Happily, Christopher met in Saint John a genius named Barlow – in a letter he described him as "a natural-born exponent of our art, with an eye for the practical use of his native timbers." Their ships were a success from the start.

Many woods were now being incorporated into New Brunswick built vessels – hackmatack (tamarack, larch), spruce, oak, white cedar, maple, beech, white elm, and not only white pine but also red pine. The masts were usually hackmatack, the yards black spruce.

Yet pine was still king. In 1824 Saint John exported 114,000 tons of pine and birch timber, 11,500,000 feet of pine boards and planks, nearly half a million pine shingles, nearly 2,000 masts and spars. Big shipments also went out from Bathurst, the Miramichi, Richibucto and St. Andrews.

New Brunswick could largely thank Napoleon for this prosperity. Colonial timber was now filling seventy-five per cent of Britain's needs. Before the great war of 1793, before Napoleon closed the Baltic, it was only one per cent.

A man of unusual vision was John S. Springer, who in the early 1830's toured pine forests in New Brunswick and Maine. He lamented the fact that the woodsman's axe and fires had already "driven this tree far back into the interior. . . . In fact the pine seems doomed, by the avarice and enterprise of white men, gradually to disappear from the borders of civilization, as have the aborigines of this country before the onward march of the Saxon race."

You find few such trees today. Yet, paradoxically, at Newcastle some magnificent pines stand guard in The Enclosure, that hushed and reverent burial ground of Miramichi pioneers, where William Davidson, the builder in 1773 of the first schooner launched on the Miramichi and the St. John River's first great exporter of masts, lies buried.

Where was spruce all this time? It was the Cinderella of the lumber family. It was slow to come into favour. Not until 1819 were the first spruce deals sawn in New Brunswick.

In the next half-century lumbering and shipbuilding flourished side by side. Great log drives were marshalled each spring on rivers like the Restigouche, St. John and Miramichi. The timber cut down during the winter was floated to the waiting mills, clustered so thick around cities and towns that their smokestacks looked like forests. By 1840, when New Brunswick's population was only 156,000, a quarter of what it is now, the province had 574 sawmills.

This was the era when stupendous tales of lumberjacks' exploits began to trickle out of the woods. A typical example is the story of how Paul Bunyan, from up Madawaska way, invented the double-bitted axe. It was an example of necessity being the mother of invention. Discouraged lumberjacks, chopping down ironwood trees on the Tobique River, complained the trunks were so tough they had to stop and re-sharpen their axe blade after each swing. Often the rebound was so violent the axe flew right out of their hands. It was a simple problem for Paul, when he happened along, walking beside his blue ox, Babe. He told the camp blacksmith to forge an axe with two blades. Then, demonstrating, he took a swipe at an ironwood tree, and with a dextrous twist of his wrists turned the axe so that on the backswing it whetted itself against an ironwood tree behind him. In this manner he always struck the tree in front with a freshly sharpened blade.

The technique proved amazingly successful. Where are the ironwood trees today, you may ask? That's just it— Paul Bunyan's system was so effective that within two years they were all cut down and now they have all disappeared.

And there were the stories of strange forest animals like the Sidehill Gouger, that extraordinary product of evolution which had two short legs on one side and two longer legs on the other, so it could run around hills in a level position.

And the endless stories about murdered lumbercamp cooks, and screams in the night, and ghostly mirages. But some of the yarns, imaginative as they may have sounded, were essentially true. For example, the one about the bizarre invasion of Maine by "Main John" Glasier, who headed a motley private expedition of New Brunswick lumberjacks armed with axes and peevees. They fought one skirmish after another until they reached the place on the Allagash River where the Americans had built a big dam that had caused the St. John River to dwindle on the Canadian side. After the angry expedition blew up the dam, the water at Grand Falls is said to have risen three feet. Main John, still wearing his formal-looking stovepipe hat on top of his luxuriant brown wig (he was balded by typhoid early in life), marched his army in triumph 160 miles back to Grand Falls.

This was the heyday of a strange and little-known fleet that called Saint John its home but was almost never home. The ships went on whale-hunting voyages to the far Pacific – voyages that might luckily be as short as a year and a half, or more likely three years, sometimes more than four years. Most seamen looked down with scorn on the "spouters," as they were called, because of the low pay, long absences, and dreary food. The masters had to be wary of the risk of deficient diets. At Galapagos they stacked big turtles between decks, six-deep, as turtles could live six months without food or water, and exercised them on deck weekly.

"They provided us with fresh messes two or three times a week," Captain Joseph G. Kenney wrote in his diary. "Thus there was no danger of scurvy among the crew, and we could remain at sea perhaps nine months."

With the constant peril of attack by wild natives of the Pacific islands, with the ever-present danger of a wounded whale turning on the small boats and splintering them with his gigantic fluke, with all the monotony between times, it might seem to have been next to impossible to enlist crews. But there were apparently always enough adventure-minded youths, disillusioned men, derelicts and fugitives to fill the complement of Saint John's seven whalers, as well as those from other New Brunswick ports.

And if you wonder how such prolonged voyages could pay for themselves, there may be a clue in the fact that one vessel alone, the *James Stewart*, during her twelve years of whaling brought home catches worth $1,500,000 to companies that produced oil for illumination and lubrication and to others that needed whalebone for umbrellas, buggy whips and corsets.

New Brunswick plunged into the shipbuilding business in a big way long before Nova Scotia. In 1843 Liverpool, England, was operating 150 ships of more than five hundred tons. Seventy-nine of these originated in New Brunswick shipyards. Another fifty-eight had come from elsewhere in Canada, mainly Quebec. Biggest of Liverpool's merchant fleet was the *Greenock*, 1,307 tons, which had slid down the launching ways at Buctouche, New Brunswick.

Yet another impetus was given to the thriving industry by two gold strikes that excited the world – in California in 1849 and in Australia in 1851. Saint John ship-owners cashed in on both. They attracted capacity passenger loads of Americans as well as Canadians anxious to get to California on advertised voyages going in 1850 via Cape Horn. And well-heeled gold miners gladly lined up to lay out nuggets for the return trips.

By now, the golden era of shipbuilding, it seemed as if giant hulls were taking form in every cove, creek, river of the New Brunswick coastline, and on all the beaches between them. You could walk the eight-hundred mile distance along the Fundy shore, up Northumberland Strait and then back along the Bay of Chaleur and rarely be out of earshot of the caulkers' mallets and the shipwrights' hammers. St. Stephen, St. Andrews, Chamcook, the Fundy islands, Saint John, Clifton, Kingston, Oromocto, St. Martins, Moncton, Dorchester, Hopewell, Sackville, Harvey Bank, Shediac, Rexton, Richibucto, Chatham, Tracadie, Caraquet, Campbellton, Bathurst, Dalhousie – virtually every city, town and village on the coast, or within sailing distance, had become a bustling shipbuilding centre.

Among the New Brunswick builders was Mrs. Edmund Powell of Richibucto, an able woman, tall, fearless and self-assertive. She had seven sons and was determined to see that they got a good education. With her sons as helpers she undertook several shipbuilding subcontracts, and then nearly floored famous lumberman and lobster canner Henry O'Leary by bidding for the main contract on his planned barque. In turn O'Leary, who knew her reputation for top-grade and punctual work, and who liked her spirit, surprised Mrs. Powell by awarding her the job. The excellent ship, named *Christina*, had a long career on the seas.

Tiny St. Martins among the red caves on the Fundy shore became known as "the village of sea captains." In a century it launched 390 brigs, brigantines, schooners, barques, barquentines, clipper ships, altogether 156,463 tons, or about two *Queen Mary* liners. Often a builder recruited a crew from sons and neighbours to sail a new vessel laden with lumber to Liverpool; there he sold both ship and cargo.

When Saint John builders and merchants turned to operating square-riggers themselves, so many thriving lines developed that the city became the fourth largest ship-owning port in the world. Biggest shipping complex in the city, and in Canada, was the Troop Line, originated by Jacob Troop from Upper Granville, Nova Scotia, and carried on by his son Howard. At its zenith it had as many as eighty-four ships ranging the world's oceans.

Often a ship-owner in rocky-landscaped Saint John would suggest to the master that if he were coming back in ballast, it might be a good idea to bring along some rich loam. Hundreds of vessels did on request; others did because they knew carts would be eager to transport ballast away from the wharf. As a result many of the residences on Mount Pleasant in Saint John are built on foreign soil. It's good earth and the flowers don't care what country it owes its allegiance to.

The craftsmen must have built the Troop windships soundly because one, at 1,769 tons the largest of the Troop line, was capable even of sailing herself. In 1888 the thirteen-year-old vessel, leaking badly after striking a coral reef during a squall, was abandoned off Guam. Supposedly a sinking derelict, the *Rock Terrace*, under lower foresails and topsail, sailed on blithely for the next five months, arousing no suspicion from passing craft. One day the German gunboat *Eber*, noticing nothing amiss, passed her. Subsequently, returning from dropping the deposed King of Samoa on one of the Marshall Islands, the *Eber* was startled to see the big ship helplessly snagged on the reefs of Tarawa. In the five months since she was abandoned the *Rock Terrace* had sailed 850 miles by herself.

But any windjammer that lived for thirteen years served her owners well and had no apologies to make, for it didn't take many voyages to repay the original cost. Look at the 1,219-ton *Star of the Sea*, a clipper built in the Wright yard at Saint John for $100,000 and sold to a Liverpool firm. She earned back her cost in three voyages on the London-Shanghai run.

And there are some who say New Brunswick's most famous vessel, the unbelievably fast clipper-type ship *Marco Polo*, made her cost with cotton in one round voyage from Liverpool to Mobile, Alabama, and back. When she was sold in the English port the proceeds were all profit. But we're getting ahead of the story . . .

The wonder of it all, looking back from this vantage point in time, is that they found mariners in 1851 brave enough to set foot on the decks of the *Marco Polo*. Any seafaring man with an eye for omens could see immediately that she was jinxed.

In those days builders didn't use complicated blueprints as they do today. A foreman shipwright whittled out a wooden half-section of the intended vessel, comprising horizontal layers that could be removed. This was what they worked from. But apparently James Smith didn't even bother to make a half-section of the *Marco Polo*. Her timbers were not shaped to any planned specifications; she was shaped to fit the surplus hackmatack timber lying about Smith's yard.

And if hers was the longest keel ever laid down in New Brunswick, it was probably only because Jim Smith had heard gossip that his Marsh Creek neighbours, the Wrights, were planning to build "a huge ship, the biggest ever, to be named the *Beejapore*, after the monster gun the British captured from the Sikhs."

Skeptics freely predicted Smith would never get his great ship out of little Marsh Creek, which dried up when the tide was out.

Hardly had the skeleton hull of the makeshift *Marco Polo* been raised when a howling Bay of Fundy gale brought the whole framework crashing down one summer night in 1850 – an ominous portent.

Jim Smith, however, was not discouraged. He started building all over again. Then, the next spring, he endured even worse agony – the launching misfired. The traditional bottle of champagne smashed against the bow – a lady's voice shrilled, "I christen this ship . . . *Marco Polo!*" – and nothing happened. They rushed up a ram of logs, but it couldn't budge her. By the time the frantic workmen located a cleat, still in place, and knocked it out, the high spring tide was going down. The gargantuan black hulk of the *Marco Polo* shivered, then slid hellbent backwards down the ways, plowing into the mud across the creek and tilting over.

Unexpectedly, two weeks later, the luck of the *Marco Polo* turned. A fortuitous high tide lifted her out of the mud. Loaded with timber, she breezed across to Liverpool, England, in fifteen days. Then she made a very speedy run to Alabama and back in thirty days.

When she was offered for sale, however, English buyers were wary. This *Marco Polo* was an odd duck, a vessel with most unorthodox lines, as fat-bellied as a dowager and with the graceful under-lines of a ballet dancer; they didn't know what to make of her. Also, she was supposed to have a "hog," a twist, in her hull as a result of the abortive launching.

But one shrewd, sharp-eyed observer knew rare quality when he saw it. Paddy McGee, a dockside rag picker and speculator, made an offer and it was accepted. Then glee-fully he brought James Baines of the ambitious young Black Ball Line down to the dock to see his prize, and Baines brought along a tough and superlatively keen master, swarthy, black-bearded Captain James Nicol (Bully) Forbes of Aberdeen, then only about thirty.

McGee didn't miss the chance to remind them, "A 'hog' has been known to increase a vessel's speed – some-times almost magically."

The quick upshot was that Baines bought the com-modious 184-foot-long ship and converted her at much expense into a queen of the Australia run. He gave her sumptuous panelled cabins and luxurious salons, yet so bulky was the *Marco Polo* that 930 passengers were accommodated, along with 60 crew, nearly 1,000 souls altogether.

On leaving, even with this great load of humanity, "Bully" Forbes exulted: "I'll have the *Marco Polo* back in the Mersey inside of six months!"

This was ridiculous; eight or nine months would be a good round-passage. Even more daringly, he bet Captain Thompson of the steam packet *Australia* he would out-race him to Melbourne.

So began one of the most memorable voyages in English-Australian marine history. "Bully" Forbes, who ashore was an austere, reserved, fine-mannered, Bible-reading layman, at sea became a fanatical driver of men and ships, exulting in danger, straining every spar, every sweep of canvas, to coax another mile out of his feverishly speeding charge. Never satisfied, he demanded more and more, until the terrified passengers protested and beseeched him to relent in the driving wind before they all went to the bottom. But Forbes, black hair streaming, standing out on the studding sail boom over the turbulent sea, was so exhilarated that he could hear only the screaming of the wind and the thunder of the sea. He roared down: "It's hell or Melbourne!"

And the *Marco Polo* bore on and on, sometimes doing as much as 336 miles a day for four days in a row. And then on September 18, only sixty-eight days out of Liverpool, she glided grandly into Port Philip Heads and dropped anchor. She had bested the steamer *Australia* by a whole week.

Immediately, there was a stampede of passengers to get to the gold fields, and Australian police rushed aboard in response to a distress signal from Captain Forbes. "I wish to have my crew kept in irons," he said blandly. "For insubordination."

Thus when he wanted to head back to England he had a ready-made crew without searching the gold fields. On October 11, Captain Forbes set forth, and sailed into Liverpool seventy-six days afterward, a week and a half ahead of the *S. S. Australia*. He had made the epic voyage to Australia and back in ten days less than six months!

And so the *Marco Polo* was embellished with a gaudy, triumphant sailcloth banner at her dock: "THE FASTEST SHIP IN THE WORLD."

Perhaps all this overstimulated Bully Forbes. He addressed passengers embarking for the second run to Australia: "Ladies and gentlemen, last trip I astonished the world with the sailing of this ship. This trip I intend to astonish God Almighty!" He didn't astonish Him, or anyone else. The ship went out in seventy-five days and came back in ninety-five, faster time than any windship except the *Marco Polo* herself, but not fast enough to equal her own record.

Bully Forbes, impelled by an insatiable lust for more and faster records, went on to other commands, and eventually became commodore of the Black Ball Line. But Fate savagely turned on him; a fine new ship gashed herself on an Australian sandbar, and although a court of inquiry acquitted Captain Forbes he never recovered from the disgrace. He skippered inconspicuous ships for the next two decades, and died at fifty-four.

You can see Forbes' tombstone at Liverpool's Smithdown Road Cemetery. The plain inscription harks back to his halcyon days:

JAMES NICOL FORBES
Late Commander of the Celebrated Clipper Ship *Marco Polo*.

His wonderful windjammer was destined to sail on for nearly another decade, outlasting one contemporary vessel after another, a symbol of the shipbuilding and designing skill of New Brunswick craftsmen. In her old age she had become a guano carrier, then, once more a lumber drogher. Her career spanned the entire greatest era of wooden shipbuilding, and only faded at the time when iron and steam were at last decisively taking over.

There are some critics who suggest today that the *Marco Polo* was never really so fleet-hulled, that the reason for her supposed swiftness was that "Bully" Forbes personally knew the right winds, the right currents, the right short-cuts. According to them, she couldn't have had an extraordinary speed-inducing "hog" in her keel anyway because she later passed marine inspections with an A-1 rating.

Well, the fact remains that other masters, less renowned, guided the *Marco Polo* to exceptionally rapid passages too. Once she logged 428 miles in a single day's sailing. No one yet knows for sure what made her go faster than other clippers built to exactly the same dimensions.

She was not by any means the only canvas-winged racer to slide down New Brunswick ways. There was the clipper *Sunda*, built by James Desmond at Chatham, which beat the celebrated American clipper *Flying Cloud* in a marathon sprint to Australia. But no ship, however able, seemed to get quite the same cap-doffing salutes from passing vessels as the proud *Marco Polo*.

Then one historic stormy day in 1883 Alex MacNeill, driving home from his forge near Cavendish, Prince Edward Island, was astonished to espy an enormous windship under billowing canvas standing in from the raging sea, just as if a blind helmsman was heading her straight for the sandy beach. "The most magnificent sight I ever saw," he said afterward.

To his even greater astonishment, he could almost swear that this was the legendary ship, the *Marco Polo*, whose initial voyage he had seen firsthand – as a seaman. He called people from far and near to hurry to the beach and watch her flying in.

What he didn't know was that the *Marco Polo*, gale-tossed in the Gulf, had sprung so many leaks she was nearly waterlogged. Her Norwegian skipper, Captain Bull, was determined to beach her in order to try to save his men's lives.

Cresting over the breakers came the massive ship, and then, three hundred yards from shore, she grounded with an agonized crunch, followed by ear-splitting crashes as her three masts cracked off into the sea.

MacNeill's lively little granddaughter watched wide-eyed at his side; the scene made a life-long impression on her memory. And later, while Captain Bull was a guest at the MacNeill home for some weeks, she gazed in wonderment as the crewmen – Norwegians, Swedes, Dutchmen, Germans, English, Scottish, Irish, Spaniards and two fuzzy-haired Tahitians – were paid off in gold sovereigns piled on the round mahogany table in the parlour.

The little girl was Lucy Maud Montgomery, one day to become internationally famous as the creator of *Anne of Green Gables*.

She recalled that throughout the several weeks that Captain Bull was a guest of her Grandfather's, she was never able to address him without casting down her eyes, as "bull" was not a name used in polite society those days.

10 Kings of the Island – and a President

Black patch over one eye, an empty gold-braided sleeve flapping in the gale, Captain William Owen, R.N., looked every inch the doughty British seadog. Fixing a telescope to his good eye, he peered across boisterous waves at a square-rigged warship coming up fast.

"*Senegal* it is!" he cried. "And a more auspicious day they could not have chosen!" He gave rapid-paced orders. Signal flags broke out suddenly overhead, naval cannon roared their salutes, a throaty sailors' cheer went up from his men.

Then Captain Owen strode down a winding flower-lined path to the jetty to greet the distinguished visitors. Oh yes . . . he wasn't on a ship, himself; he was on an island, his own island of Campobello; but he ran it like a ship.

This was 1771 – one year after the Welsh naval officer proudly led thirty-eight Lancashire settlers, including some of his former tars, across the Atlantic to begin a new life. The island had been granted to him in recompense for the loss of his right arm in the siege of Pondicherry in 1760. (His eye had been less gloriously lost in an election fight in Shrewsbury.)

On a whim, the new owner named his domain Campobello – "partly complimentary and punning on the name of the governor of the province [Sir William Campbell, whom he formerly served as secretary] and partly as applicable to the nature of the soil and the fine appearance of the island; 'Campobello' in Spanish and Italian being, I presume, synonymous to the French 'Beau Champ.' "

Before his arrival, Captain Owen had loaded himself with official documentations and licences of every possible kind "to make me formidable and respectable in my island and its neighbourhood."

It was no idle notion.

Just as a ship's master at sea was the ultimate authority in everything, Captain Owen decided the best system for Campobello would be for the island to consider itself at sea.

And so whatever needs arose, the "Principal Proprietary of the Great Outer Island of Passamaquoddy Bay" dutifully met them all. As Magistrate Owen he heard court cases; as Chaplain Owen he conducted divine service and preached; as Government Licensee Owen he issued passes to vessels and individuals leaving the province; as Government Agent Owen he drew up agreements with mainland Indian chiefs and ceremoniously quaffed *killibogus* (a mix of rum and spruce beer) to seal the bargain. He was also a prominent trader and lumber exporter. In short, a one-man Establishment who wore many hats.

One day he could be the benign benefactor, handing out choice steaks to everyone from a moose he had bought from the Indians. Then abruptly he became the seagoing disciplinarian again, ordering a pair of stocks and a whipping post erected near the market gates "to deter or punish the unruly, disorderly and dishonest."

A man who stole some rum from the store found himself ensconced in the stocks for an hour with a label pinned on his back: "A Thief, A Liar and A Drunkard."

The occasion of H.M.S. *Senegal's* arrival was doubly special to Captain Owen. The warship landed Governor Sir William Campbell, now Lord Campbell, on a visit of inspection – and with him Sir William Rich, another old friend. And Mrs. Owen had just presented her husband with a fine son.

"A general holiday!" the Principal Proprietary of Campobello happily ordained; gifts and extra pay were distributed; Rich was godfather at the christening.

Very soon after this the Owens were to leave Campobello "temporarily," the captain returning to active service because of gathering war clouds. They were never to come back. He sailed to India, commanded a warship at the second taking of Pondicherry. When he was killed in an accident at Madras in 1778 he held the rank of admiral.

More than one person has remarked through the years, "What a shame the Captain couldn't have lived to see the baby grow up and become a navy man too" – Admiral Edward William Campbell Rich Owen. Others said it wouldn't have surprised him anyway.

The more surprising thing – even more surprising than the fact that there were several admirals among William Owen's descendants and their in-laws – was that his relatively short stay in Campobello launched a feudal dynasty that was to reign well over a century.

First came a cousin, David Owen, from Wales. He was a friend of Sir Thomas Hardy of Nelson's death scene fame ("Kiss me, Hardy"), who happened to be now one of the senior British officers at nearby Eastport, Maine. David built a farmhouse which he called Tyn-e-coed, erected a church, preached in it, married people, and also obligingly played the fiddle for barn dances.

Following his death, a second navy son of the founder took over – Admiral William Fitz-William Owen, who loved the sea so much he built a duplicate of his quarterdeck over the cliff outside his new house, where he strode about in full uniform watching for spars on the horizon.

"The Quoddy Hermit," he dubbed himself.

To say the new Principal Proprietary possessed a complex character would be an understatement. He was both vain and religiously humble, self-centered and generous, arrogant and courtly. He loved ceremonies, a hearty guffaw, and courting the ladies, although not essentially in that order.

Some of his inner conflicts might have originated in an unsettled boyhood. He was Captain Owen's illegitimate son, who, at five, when asked what his last name was, replied, "I don't know, but if you want to know you may ask Mother – she can tell you." Buffeted about, brought up in several homes, often punished, he took solace in wearing a brave-looking cocked hat and a suit of scarlet made from an old coat of his late father's. He only gradually learned about his navy father.

The boy followed in his footsteps, won distinction and the friendship of Nelson, and on retiring to Campobello brought a host of mementos including two cannon from a captured Spanish galleon. These he placed on a promontory to warn off American fishermen, removing the armament only twice each year–to fire a salute to the Queen's Birthday and to open the fish fair.

"The Quoddy Hermit" lived somewhat more elegantly – and more gregariously – than most recluses. There were ornate coaches, glittering chandeliers, ubiquitous servants, choice wines. His frequent invitations to friends to drop in for a meal meant an elaborate game dinner at four, tea at seven, a rubber of whist until nine, scripture reading and worship and then, after the ladies took their leave, good cigars, whiskey and war-reminiscing into the small hours.

Like his predecessors, Admiral William Fitz-William shirked no obligations of office. As Lord of the Manor he was host at formal balls. As Overseer of the Poor he took food baskets to the needy. When cash was scarce he accepted fish and game as rent. Finally he solved the money problem by setting up his own bank and issuing one dollar promissory certificates embellished with his family crest and motto, *Flecti Non Frangi* ("To be bent, not to be broken.") This apparently saved the island from going broke when remittances from England were slow. He graciously consented to be patron for a theatrical performance, then composed the songs for it. He preached and baptized, often leaving out any sections of the liturgy that he didn't happen to like. He also married couples – and invariably insisted on claiming the first kiss of the bride.

Once a sailor being married to a Campobello girl, determined to thwart this well-known custom, turned and reached out for her as the last sentence was being intoned.

"You are not married yet. Back!" bellowed the admiral.

Red-faced, the young man snapped to attention. Slowly the admiral repeated the final words " . . . pronounce . . . you . . . man . . . and . . . " – moving toward the bride – ". . . wife," said the admiral, and grabbed her.

But after his death in 1857 you could see the Owens' domination fading. In the early 1860's Captain Robinson Owen campaigned vigorously up and down the island on the theme: "Confederation would be disaster." When the voting was held, Campobello went for Confederation by a landslide.

The dynasty lasted until 1881, when American interests purchased a large part of Campobello to develop as a resort for wealthy Americans.

Two years later a Delaware and Hudson Railway vice-president, spending a family vacation at the new Tyn-e-coed Hotel on the site of David Owen's old farm, was struck by the panoramic ocean view from a house then under construction. James Roosevelt promptly bought the house and four acres, and brought his wife, Sarah, and their baby son, Franklin, back next year to become summer residents.

It was on this ruggedly beautiful Canadian island – a geographical anomaly, separated from Lubec in Maine by only a narrow tide-rip, but forty-five miles by highway from the Canadian mainland – that a future president of the United States was to spend much of his next thirty-seven years. It was here that Franklin learned to fish, hunt, swim, paddle, sail, make speeches, debate politics; here that he brought his bride on their honeymoon; and here he built a golf course which didn't inconvenience any of his neighbours because the farmers continued to graze their sheep on it anyway.

And it was here, that fateful day in 1921, after he had given sailing lessons to his small sons, helped to fight a forest blaze and then enjoyed an icy dip, that Franklin Roosevelt sat in his wet bathing suit reading the latest arrived newspapers and was seized by chills and a mysterious, crippling illness. It was not diagnosed as infantile paralysis until fifteen days later.

They carried him away on a stretcher, a permanently stricken man – and he returned twelve years later, accompanied by warships and all the mighty panoply of the presidency of the United States.

It was a fine June day in Welchpool as the schooner *Amberjack II* glided up to the crowded wharf. The helmsman in the breeze-tossed Panama hat waved and flashed his familiar smile, and people wildly applauded and yelled greetings and waved back.

Obviously the islanders stood in no such awe of the president of the United States as their forefathers did of the legendary Owens. They affectionately looked upon Franklin Roosevelt, not as the prestigious leader of the most powerful nation on earth, but as one of their own come back at last.

"Welcome home, Frank boy!" one of the old fishermen shouted, and the helmsman shouted back, calling him by name.

No one looked more radiantly happy than Franklin Roosevelt, for Campobello to him was always "the beloved island." He was glad to be home, glad to have the chance to welcome life-long friends at the Roosevelt "cottage" – the red-shingled Dutch colonial mansion of thirty-four rooms which had been his mother's wedding gift to Franklin and Eleanor – and glad to be able to enjoy a beach picnic again, with Mrs. Roosevelt kneeling as she roasted hot dogs on a long fork.

But it was not quite like the old days, with coded messages chattering in all night on the world monetary crisis; nor was it ever to be again. Franklin Roosevelt in his remaining twelve years managed only two trips back, in 1936 and 1939, and the final visit lasted only a few hours.

Campobello in 1946 erected the first memorial to Franklin D. Roosevelt outside the United States – a gleaming cairn of New Brunswick red granite, just outside the tiny, weathered public library of which he had been honorary president.

They called the new bridge after him too – the Franklin D. Roosevelt International Bridge – when the two countries at long last linked Campobello to the mainland.

And then Canada and the United States agreed jointly to establish a resort unique in the whole world – the Roosevelt Campobello International Park, centred on the twenty-acre Roosevelt estate – both as a tribute and a symbol of good neighbourliness. It is to become a conference centre on international co-operation and goodwill.

A cavalcade of notables came to help launch the park; first Mrs. Lyndon B. Johnson and Mrs. Lester B. Pearson to dedicate it; later the Queen Mother, and Prime Minister Pearson and President Johnson to lay the cornerstone for the reception centre.

The park has grown to 3,000 acres, encompassing four other great "cottages." Now a steady stream of summertime humanity files through the unpretentious, plainly furnished rooms of Roosevelt's house, feeling the nostalgic thrill of seeing all the accoutrements still in place – his sea charts, his weathered telescope, the megaphone with which he used to hail boats, or call the family to meals, the flag presented to him by Congress, the Presidential Emblem, a picture of a sailboat he painted as a youngster, the oars he plied at Harvard, the chair he sat in while presiding over his first cabinet meeting. On the wall there is a framed letter from young Franklin to his mother saying what he wanted for Christmas, and at the reception centre, a birchbark canoe made by Passama-quoddy Indian, Tomah Joseph, the same canoe that the handsomely stalwart young Roosevelt is paddling in one of his most memorable photographs.

Campobello today, as ever, is an unbelievably tranquil refuge where you picnic on a grassy headland and watch fishing craft silently ghosting by like toy boats on a glass mirror . . . where Canadians talk in a slow Maine coast drawl without an "r" in "a cah-load," but remain defin-itely, even militantly, Canadian . . . where an old fellow with a sack on his back may come up to your parked car and ask whether you would like to take some fresh mack-erel home to the mainland, (he's a scoop man in a fish-packing plant and they can't use the mackerel) and then he'll surprise you by resolutely refusing to take anything for the fish . . . where a housewife answers the doorbell and gives you directions and replies offhandedly when you thank her, "That's all right, dear" . . . where the old 1835 home of the peppery lady's man Admiral William Fitz-William Owen still stands on Deer Point and counts among its more recent house-guests the lovely (if somewhat belated) Greer Garson, when she came for the filming of *Sunrise At Campobello* . . . where you may notice two happy-go-lucky nondescript-looking characters in rainjackets and old pants, setting forth on a fisherman's motorboat in a squall to visit Penguin Island, and be sur-prised to learn they are both members of the Roosevelt Campobello International Park Commission, men to whom this place is very close. One is genial, quiet Senator Edmund S. Muskie, former governor of next-door Maine. The other, his face lit up by a smile in the F.D.R. mould, is Franklin D. Roosevelt Jr., to whom Campobello bears a greater significance than merely that of a summer-colony: this is where he was born.

If you would really like to understand how Campobello people still regard Franklin Roosevelt Sr. – as very much one of themselves, rather than as a renowned chief of state

– all you need do is glance at the bronze plaque placed on the back pew in St. Anne's Anglican Church, the pew he sat in. It says, quite truthfully:

To The Glory Of God
In Memory Of
Franklin Delano Roosevelt
1882-1945
Honorary Vestryman of
St. Anne's Church

11 Lobsters that Fly, Birds that Walk on Water, Men who Walk on Trees

Far down the dim corridors of time – long before Champlain and deMonts established on St. Croix Island the first European settlement on the Atlantic coast north of Florida – did white men live in the Passamaquoddy Bay region?

Unquestionably the great French explorers of 1604 were preceded by transient fishermen and traders – French, Basque, Portuguese and others, who carefully sketched the Bay of Fundy on their maps in the 1500's.

Reportedly Champlain and deMonts realized this anew when they met Chief Chkoudun at Menagoueche (Saint John). They did not know for sure – so the legend goes – whether any European ever set foot ashore here before. But the chief didn't seem taken aback to see them; and he seemed to catch on surprisingly fast to the idea of bartering fur pelts for beads and baubles, cloth and knives.

When Champlain was departing, he waved happily to Chief Chkoudun and said: "Adieu!"

Replied Chkoudun, waving back: "Adios!"

But five centuries before – was the Passamaquoddy region the "Straumey" of the Norse explorers? Was it here that Thorfinn Karlsifini's wife bore him a son – the first white native of all North America?

Some researchers are convinced. They claim the island of Grand Manan is unmistakably in the Norse descriptions; so are the tidal eddies and whirlpools off Deer Island.

Passamaquoddy Indian lore tells of a strange tribe

from afar known as the Caansoos, that lived there in the long-ago and then "vanished into the earth." This could have been how it seemed to the Red Men after the expedition – 160 Norsemen and their womenfolk – loaded their cattle aboard three ships and sailed back to Greenland.

Some extraordinary parallels exist between Passamaquoddy Indian legends and Norse sagas. Did the primitive Indians borrow theirs from the story-loving Norsemen? Or, as a number of historians believe, did the Norse adventurers adapt Indian folktales to their own use?

But wait – have I given the impression that with tide-rips and whirlpools, it must be an exciting sea voyage out to visit Deer Island? The surprising thing, when you arrive at l'Étang to drive aboard the ferry, is to find there is no sea voyage at all – Deer Island is little more than a stone's skip from the mainland; it's like crossing a harbour.

But it's a fascinating short trip. Your ferry is a shallow-bottomed craft with a low upper deck – a plebian boat that looks as if it always wanted to a Mississippi riverboat – and because the deck is close to the water you feel that you are skimming along on an air-cushioned Hovercraft. Effortlessly the ferry threads its way in and around tiny evergreen-capped islands and through wraith-like wisps of fog, for it has radar eyes.

Then an undulating trip over a roller-coaster road – full of dips familiarly known as "thank-you-mams" – and suddenly we arrive at a unique sea farm, the biggest lobster pound in the world.

Half a dozen tidal inlets on Deer Island and Grand Manan have been converted into similar corrals – their salt water naturally changed twice a day by the surging inrush of the mighty twenty-eight-foot Fundy tides, controlled by dams and sluice gates. Without continual refreshing of the water, the lobsters would quickly die from lack of oxygen.

Within the great arena-like fishbowl of weathered grey slats and wire netting, somewhere far below the murky waters, are 500,000 pounds of live lobsters in their workday shell coats of blackish-greenish hue. If need be, twice as many could crawl around and not crowd each other. They are fed two pounds of herring daily for each one hundred pounds of lobsters.

The reason for these permanent marine ranches is simple: Canada enforces district season limits on trapping lobsters. By buying them here and there in regular seasons and putting them in the pounds alive, the St. Andrews shippers find it possible to send them almost anywhere, anytime, on demand. Huge, dripping refrigerator-trucks filled with live lobsters, seaweed and ice rumble toward the American border. And live lobsters, packed in sawdust or dried wood shavings are flown from Saint John and Moncton by four-engine jet freightliners to distribution centres in Europe.

One day in the ancient Roman city of Trier, West Germany, close to the Luxembourg frontier, I was served a lobster cocktail in the hotel diningroom.

It was so tasty I couldn't help complimenting the head-waiter, almost in envy.

"I knew nothing previously of your lobsters," I said, "but these are really very good. Did they come from the North Sea area – from Hamburg or Bremen?"

"From Hamburg," he replied. "But first they were flown from eastern Canada."

Deer Island is also a place with an age-old tradition of skilled shipbuilding. On the Richardson ways, for instance, you may find a wooden fishing boat taking form side by side with a sleek yacht for a Connecticut sportsman. The favourable dollar exchange rate and low United States duty mean that many Americans do much better building boats in the Maritimes than at home.

Here, too, just off the shore you see many herring weirs (called "wares" by fishermen) that invariably intrigue inlanders. They're giant, fenced-in circular traps – often more than an acre in size – walled in the old days by intertwined brush, now by nylon twine netting, fastened to stakes driven into the sea bed. The herring follow their noses along the lead-in wall through a funnel-like entrance and then mill around within the great enclosure unable to find their way out again.

Gathered up inside the weir by a purse-seine, the herring are pumped aboard sardine carriers by a suction so gentle that the fishermen say it won't break eggs. "Scale boats" collect the silvery scales from the carriers, in exchange for the pumping chore.

The shiny scales are a substantial business in themselves – they're sold to pearl-essence plants in New England to impart lustre to artificial pearls, varnish, and plastics. Meanwhile the sardines go to canning factories in Maine and New Brunswick – including the Connors Brothers plant at Black's Harbour, New Brunswick, which ranks as the biggest in the Commonwealth. Unwanted groundfish are shipped to pet food canneries in Maine.

On a good tide, a weir produces a catch of two hundred hogsheads, or nearly half a million herring. That's a lot of fish; but it also costs a lot to build a weir these days – up to $12,000 – and a sudden Fundy storm can wreck the investment in minutes. And weir-boats today are not just wooden shells. Most have ship-to-shore phones to keep contact with buyers, also electronic depth-sounding devices to detect schools of fish when purse-seining out in the bay, as well as radar for navigating.

On balance, the fishermen seem to come out of it not too badly. Many a summer visitor has remarked that a returning fisherman may be wearing rough clothes, and his rubber boots may be flecked like glitter-dust with herring scales, but when he picks up his morning paper he turns first to the financial page.

Along miles of Deer Island coastline in the early 1920's walked a man who stopped often to stare out to sea and to the mainland and nearby Campobello – a man who was seeing not endless waves, nor ships, nor fish, but instead mammoth concrete walls. These, in his imagination, formed a system of dams and seagates, creating two vast basins, one in Passamaquoddy Bay and one in Maine's Cobscook Bay.

It was an extremely ambitious dream that gripped Dexter P. Cooper – and as it turned out, at least in his time, an impossible dream.

This American hydraulic engineer wanted to harness the tremendous tides of the Bay of Fundy – the 170 mile-long sea enclave in which more than 100 billion tons of water swell and recede each day, a demonstration of natural power unsurpassed in the world. When the moon's pull is at its strongest, the tides at the head of the bay may rise and drop as much as fifty-three feet – a circumstance due to the combined effect of the tides themselves, the pulsating wave rhythm from the sea in the funnel-shaped bay, and the upward-sloping bay bottom that carries the incoming tide level ever higher.

From earliest recorded history the coves near the head of the bay have served as natural dry docks, where repairs could be made to the hulls of tied up fishing vessels while they stood, like fish out of water, high and dry on mudflats when the tide was out. Similarly, fishermen drove out with horse and wagon to harvest the catch from the weirs, having to reach high over their heads with rakes to get pollock, haddock, cod and shad down out of the netting.

The visionary Mr. Cooper set up corporations in Canada and the United States to spearhead the power development, ran into opposition from Canadian fishing interests, revised his plans to convert the project to all-American scope, enlisted the enthusiastic support of his Campobello neighbour, President Roosevelt, then saw the fledgling Quoddy scheme die when Congress balked at further government spending on it. Crux of the controversy: whether Quoddy could ever produce power more cheaply than it could be generated by other means.

Brief flurries of interest have arisen since, particularly during President Kennedy's administration, but the anticipated million daily kilowatts of Quoddy electric power are still a-wasting in the rampaging tides, along with several millions of dollars spent by Washington, and about a third of a million dollars spent by the late, disillusioned Mr. Cooper.

Nobody in the Bay of Fundy islands realized more keenly than Allan Moses of Grand Manan the tragedy of humanity's indifference to the survival of wildlife. An unassuming man, with the bristling black mustache of a British Army captain, Moses was a "natural naturalist"; as a youth he was so imbued with the desire to study the creatures of the world around him that he abandoned his advanced education.

He knew about the affluent English sports who came to New Brunswick in the 1800's to shoot caribou – stodgy, passive targets that obligingly herded themselves together to be gunned down at leisure – as many as thirty or forty at a time for the sheer fun of it. The carcasses were left to rot; and now the caribou were gone.

He knew about the phenomenal angling enjoyed by army officers in early times – such incredibly lively fishing that sometimes two and three lake trout leaped up for the hooks during the *back*-cast of the fishing line. Now you didn't catch many fish accidentally.

He knew of the precipitate decline of the passenger pigeon, that eating delicacy batted down out of the air by long poles swung by hunters hiding behind hilltops. It was no bother for anyone to fill a few barrels because these thunderous migrating flocks darkened the sky for as long as twelve hours at a time. Everyone was surfeited. In cases where household servants were engaged on a contract basis, it was often stipulated that passenger pigeon could not be served more than twice a week. By 1915 the species was extinct.

Moses knew walrus had once been plentiful at Point Miscou in the northeast of New Brunswick, and at Portage Island in Miramichi Bay, and even at Shediac. Now they were no closer than Labrador.

He knew wolves had roamed so freely over New Brunswick during the mid-1800's that lumberjacks at camp in Charlotte County reported seeing thirty to forty wolves looking down at them around the edge of the open roof where the smoke went out. Near Bath in the 1840's Mrs. Elizabeth Squires, grandmother of New Brunswick naturalist W. A. Squires, walked into a pack of eight wolves on a country road at dusk. It didn't faze her. "Shoo!" she said, and they fled into the woods. She thought until then they were sheep. Now wolves had been missing from the province for nearly a century.

There were still lots of sea birds, of course. For them, Grand Manan was a migratory flight terminal that saw a never-ending stream of air traffic coming and going. But the day was past when a group such as Captain William Owen of Campobello, his guests and a band of Indians could round up thousands of ducks and other waterfowl in a creek at St. Andrews and massacre seven hundred in a single orgy of paddle-wielding and not make a dent in the local feathered population.

Some seafowl, like the Labrador ducks, the Eskimo curlews and the long-billed curlews, had become either extremely scarce, or extinct over the years. And it greatly worried Allan Moses to know that the eider ducks of the

Bay of Fundy – the loveliest of all sea duck species – were now vanishing.

Then, unexpectedly, fate stepped in – or rather, flew in. In the form of a strange bird Grand Manan had never seen before.

Like Wrong-Way Corrigan, the airman who was supposed to fly across the United States, but instead winged out over the Atlantic, a mollymauk inexplicably flew northward from the Equator instead of southward.

The big bird was shot off Southern Head, Grand Manan, by Ernest Joy. It was one of the first times a Yellow-Nosed Mollymauk, a member of the albatross family, had been known to venture into the Northern Hemisphere.

Mr. Joy gave his prize to Allan Moses, and Mr. Moses duly mounted it for his little personal natural history museum at North Head, into which patrons walked through an archway formed by the jaw-bone of a whale.

Soon an intense interest was shown by the American Museum of Natural History in acquiring the bird. Allan Moses turned down repeated offers. Then on a whim he made a counter-proposal: he'd trade his Yellow-Nosed Mollymauk for a chance to serve as taxidermist on an expedition to Africa.

So he found himself en route to German East Africa with the J. Sterling Rockefeller party to search for the extremely rare Green Broadtail, a member of the family of African Fly-catchers. Only one had ever been taken before – by a native who sold it to an Austrian named Grauer, who, in turn, sold it to the Rothschild Collection in London.

The quest was a failure . . . that is, right up to the last day. Then Allan Moses, lying on his cot fighting a recurrence of malaria, espied a green broadtail – of all things – sitting on a tree branch just outside the jungle tent. He shot it.

J. Sterling Rockefeller was so elated that later, when he heard Allan Moses remark glumly, "It would cost less than the $150,000 price-tag of this expedition to save the eider ducks of the Bay of Fundy," he promptly purchased their breeding ground, Kent Island, six miles off Grand Manan. He presented it to Bowdoin College of Maine, and for decades now Bowdoin's "Outpost of Science" has been a focus of research on many species of sea birds besides the thriving eider ducks.

These include Leach's petrels, or Mother Carey's Chickens, the little, dark-grey ocean wanderers that winter in the Azores, 4,000 miles away and, returning by night, zero unerringly into the self-same underground burrows they occupied last year. They flit back to Kent Island despite the fact that their 10,000 population on the narrow two-mile-long island is exceeded five-to-one by America's largest breeding concentration of herring gulls, who love to eat them like peanuts.

Kent Island, in fact, is alive with gulls. They're so numerous the 150-acre expanse looks whiter than white. Because myriads of gulls perch on the spruces and firs, the trees grow into stunted flat-tops, vaguely resembling a Japanese landscape, and a man can easily walk around on the platforms.

Bowdoin scientists are gradually unravelling the behavioural secrets of Mother Carey's Chickens. They report there is no basis in fact for the folk tale that the birds, when weary, float on their backs and use their wings as sails. Nor is it true that they carry their eggs under their wings in flight and hatch them at sea. But they do, in a sense, walk on water, flittering along on their webbed feet as they take off – also, almost imperceptibly, using their fast-moving wing-tips as water-skiing poles.

But as Bowdoin biologist Dr. Charles E. Huntington points out, many questions remain. For example: Why do they lay only one egg a year? How do they find their way back to a tiny island in a thick fog on a moonless night? And once there, how do they find their own burrow in the midst of the woods?

In the hope of getting answers, the ornithologists spy on them in the dark with infra-red "snooperscopes," band them and trace them, spin them on a record-player turntable, subject them to a strong electromagnetic field. It's hardly surprising if Leach's petrels don't seem anxious to be close friends with humans.

On Kent and close-by islands you find also the puffin, whose vividly coloured parrot bill and "eyeglasses" give him a clown look; the black guillemot, which nests deep in the crevices between big rocks; the razor-billed auk, a relative of the extinct great auk; and several varieties of gulls.

Like so many other parts of New Brunswick, Kent

Island has its own legend of tragedy. John Kent, an English pioneer, apparently had a happy life there in the 1700's; yet his widow became a recluse, an aging and ugly crone who prophesied no one would live on the island after her death.

One day as an English brig approached the fateful Murr Ledges in dense fog, the rum-sodden master insisted he take the wheel himself because he had seen a witch in a vision who said, "Follow my directions and you can sail right through the reefs." Soon the vessel came to a lurching, grinding halt, badly holed on the jutting rocks, and began to fill fast. As survivors reached the only home on the Kent shore, the bleary captain was shaken when the door creaked open and he beheld the lone occupant. "That woman!" he whispered hoarsely to his mate as they warmed themselves by the fire. "She was the witch who led me here!"

On Grand Manan, a generation ago, three hundred smokehouses transformed big silvery herring into the golden-tanned cured fish that were shipped out in wooden boxes to the United States, Caribbean and South America. There were so many smokehouses that the haze of their sawdust-dampened spruce log fires made villages look from a distance as if they were ablaze. Off the coast you could count more than a hundred weirs, stationary fish traps. Now there are only about six smokehouses, only twenty-five licenced weirs.

This reflects not a decline in fishing so much as a change in markets and tastes, and a revolution in fishing methods. Today they don't wait for the fish to come in. Electronically-equipped fleets – altogether 175 craft ranging from small purse seiners to large draggers, or one for every fifteen residents of the island – go out to track down the schools. The ships use modern echo-sounders and radar, and ship-to-shore radiophones to keep in touch with dealers.

One thing hasn't changed – nearby are what are claimed to be the richest lobster grounds in the Atlantic. Grand Manan has several natural lobster pounds on its sheltered east side, in the vicinity of a strange "submarine forest" of huge tree stumps under the ocean water. By contrast, the forbidding western side, of volcanic origin, is so precipitous that its three hundred-foot-high walls looked like the Alps to famed ornithologist and bird artist, John James Audubon, when he approached the island on a visit in 1833.

The only sizeable break in the cliffs on this uninhabited west coastline is Dark Harbor where bald eagles soar and wheel overhead – the cove that makes Grand Manan the dulse capital of the world.

As every New Brunswicker on the Fundy coast knows, dulse is an edible seaweed, flat, sometimes pink-soft, and sometimes purple-shiny and leathery, picked from rocks at low tide and dried in the sun for five hours. The taste is salty and tangy. A baby in Spokane or Esquimault allowed to lick a strip of dulse will always remain a true New Brunswicker at heart, no matter how many miles separate him from the Atlantic Coast.

Experienced pickers can gather 125 pounds before the dulse rocks are again inundated; and of course there is another low tide later that day or night. Total annual harvest at Grand Manan is 150,000 pounds, dried weight. Reinforcing the insistent demand from Maritimers and former Maritimers – who eat dulse raw, toast it over a candle flame, or add it in powdered form to clam chowder, fish casserole, beef ragout, or gravy – is a new market among health-store chains, which sell dulse in capsules because it is rich in iodine, iron and other nutrients.

The unwrapping of a twenty-pound carton of this seaweed at a Maritimers' reunion in Vancouver or Los Angeles is always guaranteed to trigger a bigger riot than the arrival of Jane Fonda.

Connoisseurs can tell immediately, from the look and taste of dulse, whether it came from Grand Manan or from Maces Bay on the mainland – they all crave their own special kind, and can't stop eating it until the bag is empty. A store display-window full of dulse in Saint John always attracts a knot of puzzled inland tourists. A typical comment: "Can't say for dead certain, but I think it's insulating material." His serious-looking friend's reply: "I'd say stable litter."

One rare American took an instant liking to dulse, loaded up his car trunk with it, then sat bewildered in a United States customs office at an inland border point for some time while officials, who had never seen dulse before, pondered whether it was marijuana.

When you're tired of picking dulse, you can dig for Captain Kidd's booty at Money Cove, two miles north of Dark Harbor. The instructions obligingly left by the buccaneer are easy: the location of two kegs of gold is marked by two French willows. But since then, French willows have proliferated all over the place.

To the north again is deserted Indian Beach, where braves formerly came to shoot porpoises and gather pipestone to carve. One reason it's deserted: people on shore and on ships have reported seeing the flaming ghost of an Indian squaw, a brilliant human torch, walking across the beach. She materializes during violent weather, and her appearance heralds impending catastrophe.

Because fifteen mile-long Grand Manan is twenty-five miles from New Brunswick and only six miles from Maine, the American influence is strong. Once there was a saying that you could identify anyone from the north or south of the island by his accent; the southern residents had a more distinct New England twang.

So this is Grand Manan; where time, tide and the elements have sculptured high, sharply chiselled rock statues known by such distinctive names as The Bishop and Southern Cross; where American authoress, Willa Cather wrote several of her novels at her Whale Cove cottage; where the name of the original 1784 settler, Loyalist Moses Gerrish, a Harvard alumnus, is perpetuated by the history-minded Gerrish House Society, whose centennial project was the new Grand Manan Museum at Grand Harbor; where amidst the sea-moist air European flowers bloom in such luxuriance as to out-rival a Swiss mountain meadow; where the most heroic exploit was the feat of James Lawson, a seaman from the square-rigger *Lord Ashburton*, which, in a screaming blizzard in 1857, was driven all the way from within sight of her Saint John destination to Grand Manan and there wrecked. Lawson miraculously clawed his way at night, in the freezing storm, up the sheer face of the three hundred-foot Seven Days' Work cliffs to find rescue for himself and his surviving shipmates. Six of them were found sitting with their heads down on their knees and could not be awakened. They had frozen to death.

It's odd: in contrast with the 1800's when they merely sat home and tended their weirs, and attached scythe blades to the hulls of their doreys to row out and devastate the nets of the intruding New England fishermen, the Grand Manan fishermen today are themselves the venturers with their superbly equipped vessels – and they in turn have been fired on as intruders by weir fishermen at St. Mary's Bay, Nova Scotia.

As they glide home with their big catches, they have reason to be grateful to a fellow Grand Mananer, Dr. Ernest W. Guptill, head of the physics department at Dalhousie University in Halifax. It happened that he discovered the "eyes" of radar. Developed during the Second World War, it was first used in the bellies of Lancaster Pathfinder bombers. Now you can see it rotating above the wheelhouses of countless thousands of ships around the world – including Guptill's home island's modern fishing fleet.

12 What's in a Name?

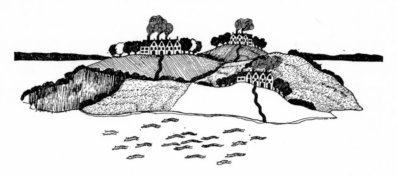

Almost everyone makes the same guess about how Dochet's Island (pronounced "Doe-shay's") on the Canadian-American border got its name: "Easy! From a Frenchman named Dochet."

But no. This little spot in the St. Croix River between New Brunswick and Maine, now an American national historic site – once known as Bone Island, Boon Island, Neutral Island, called by the Indians "Mut-an-ag-wes," or "A place to leave things," a place where thirty-five of the seventy-nine men in Champlain's and deMonts' pioneer expedition left their skeletons that tragic 1604-5 winter – was named for a pretty English-speaking girl.

"Dosia" was the nickname of Theodosia Milberry, daughter of a clergyman from Bayside, New Brunswick. She set tongues wagging by rowing her boy friend to the island for trysts among the mouldering graves. The scandal made such an impression that it's still commemorated in the name two centuries later.

Let's trace down Geary, the name of a village, and also the name of the woods between Saint John and Fredericton. This also should be easy: there are still Geary families in southern New Brunswick. But if you look back to 1811 maps the name is spelled Gary, and in the late 1700's it was New Niagary, a village founded by United Empire Loyalists who came from the United States via Niagara, Ontario. They added a colloquial "y" in the same way pioneers called Iowa "Ioway."

Similarly, Tanty-Wanty, the name of a small stream a few miles from Geary, is baffling until you realize there is a similar stream, called the Tanawanda, a few miles from Niagara, Ontario.

Names evolve very oddly sometimes. "Menagoeuche," the Indian word for Saint John, survives today in two far-out forms, Manawagonish Road and nearby Mahogany Island.

Few parts of North America can even approach the flavour of New Brunswick's nomenclature, especially when you include the mellifluous and often tongue-defying Maliseet and Micmac Indian words, which native New Brunswickers roll off their tongues effortlessly.

Kouchibouguac, Magaguadavic, Pocowogamis, Washademoak, Kennebecasis, Digdeguash, are some of the shorter ones – shorter, that is, in comparison with Mermerimammericook and those two St. John River tributaries which seemingly anticipated the snowmobile era, the Skoodawabskoosis and the Skoodawabskook. Another fascinating word is the Indian name for Portage Island in Miramichi Bay: Mogulaweechooacadie, which sounds like a sneeze and means, simply, "A place where brant geese are plentiful and they are generally shot, as it were."

There are synthetic Indian names, laboriously devised by white men for rural railway stations – like Penobsquis ("stone" and "brook"), Plumweseep ("salmon" and "river"), Quispamsis ("lake" and "little").

There are bumbling attempts to go native, like the stretches of river named "Long Lookum" on the St. Croix, Upsalquitch and Nepisiguit. And hybrid names, like Pokomoonshine.

In fact there's something for everyone. You can exclaim approvingly over names like Temperance Vale and Teetotal Settlement, or moisten your lips at the sight of Brandy Brook, Brandy Cove, Brandy Point, Five Fingers, Grog Brook, Old Proprietor Shoal, Whiskey Island, and two Gin Brooks.

The aroma of the Middle East wafts in with names like Jerusalem, Goshen, Bagdhad, Balm of Gilead Cove, Zion, Damascus.

You can teach children to count on One-Mile Brook, Two Rivers Inlet, Three Corner Lake, Four Roads, Five Fathom Hole, Six Roads, Seven Days' Work, Eight-Mile Gulch, Nine-Mile Brook. Or start your own menagerie with Flea Island, Bull Moose Hill, Wildcat Brook, Bear

Trap Point, Roaring Bull, Camel Back Mountain, Boars Back Hill, Rat Tail Brook.

However, for sheer colour it's hard to beat Barnaby's Nose Brook, Half Moon, Push-and-Be-Damned Rapids, Jack Tars Cove, Tinkettle Brook, Oven Head, Trousers Lake, Taxes River, Yankee Brook, Big Hovel Brook, Outhouse Point, Big John Brook, Diggity Cove, Coronary Lake, Deadman's Harbour, Crazy Lake, Fly Tent Brook, Humbug Brook, Cigar Falls Brook, Fatpot Island, Blowdown Settlement, Cannonball Island, Devil's Elbow, Jail Island, Gallows Hill, Burnt Church, Doughboy Brook, Zachie Jonah Mountain, Juvenile Settlement, Grindstone Rock, Malcontents River, Spit Shoal, Hecklars' Cove, Iron Bound Cove, Zephyr Rock, not to mention Keyhole Lake, Love Lake and Mates Corner.

You'll frequently be fooled by names that aren't what they seem to be. Who would doubt that Belleisle River was named for a lovely island, or that Beauséjour in Westmorland County perpetuates a fine day and a beautiful vista? Yet both were named after French pioneers. For instance, Alexander LeBorgne de Belleisle, descendant of the storied Charles de la Tour and his second wife, was living on the St. John River in 1754. His two daughters married Robichand brothers who settled near by, and from one of these families Premier Louis J. Robichand is a direct descendant.

Bonny River bears no resemblance to Scotland; it was named for Joel Bonny, a pre-Loyalist settler.

Bull's Creek is a creek with no bull; it was called after Loyalist Lieutenant George Bull.

Coldbrook was never what it seems to say; it honoured Governor Sir William Colebrook of New Brunswick.

Bon Ami Point isn't a commercial; it was named for Peter Bonamy, a grantee in the late 1790's.

Dipper Harbour isn't shaped like a dipper; it was called after a type of duck that dips when catching its prey.

Glasier Lake has no more ice than the next one; it was named for The Honourable John Glasier.

Fox Island – you guessed it – has no foxes. The origin of the name is Charles James Fox, minister to George III.

And Indiantown, in Saint John's North End, has no Indians. It was the site of a trading outpost erected in 1779.

Kill-Me-Quick Rips, those fearsome-sounding rapids on the St. Croix, aren't likely to. The name is a corruption of the Indian "Kilmaquac."

St. Stephen sounds sanctimonious; perhaps isn't. Some say "saint" was prefixed to the Christian name of a member of the original surveying party.

Pope's Folly has no relation to the Pontiff. Two Passamaquoddy Bay islands bear this name, after a Mr. Pope who established a trading post and then lost everything.

The English, as is known, have a tendency to Anglicize French and Indian names, or at least find plausible explanations for them. What an unmistakably English-sounding name is Kedgwick, the northern river sometimes called the Tom Kedgwick! But it isn't. In 1818 it appeared under the French name of "Madame Kiswic" on the map. Earlier it was pure Indian "Memkeswee." In the Shepody district you may hear that its name comes from Chapeau Dieu, or God's hat, an allusion to Shepody Mountain, or in Tormentine that this name stemmed from the torments caused by mosquitoes. Midgic, similarly, came from midgets, Quaco from the racket of quacking ducks, Portobello from the hallooing of a man named Porter lost in the woods, Nauwigewauk from the question asked by an Indian of his weary squaw resting by the roadside: "Now would'ja walk?"

All of them are wrong.

Then there's Yoho. Does it make you think of a bottle of rum? You mightn't be too far astray. Historian Dr. W. F. Ganong remarked soberly that the unusual name of this lake, fifteen miles from Fredericton, apparently resulted from "some incident in the survey made in 1810." It was listed on the maps then as "Yahoo."

But interpretations of historical names, unfortunately, are often completely contradictory. As a native Saint Johnner I was delighted to read one historian's report that "Menagoueche," the ancient Indian name for Saint John, meant "The Place Of Mighty People." Then another historian's report: For some unknown reason the Indians called the city "Men-ak-wes," meaning "Where They Collect The Dead Seals."

As I said, there's something for everybody.

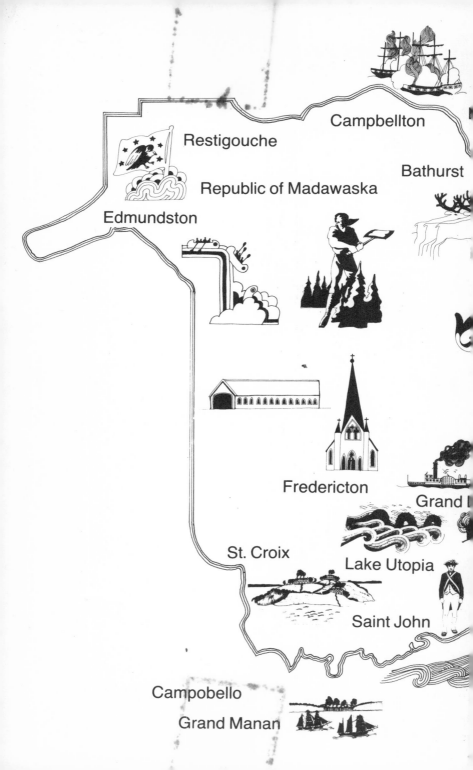

Campbellton

Restigouche

Bathurst

Republic of Madawaska

Edmundston

Fredericton

Grand

St. Croix

Lake Utopia

Saint John

Campobello

Grand Manan